SOME OF ME

SOME OF ME

Isabella Rosselli

RANDOM HOUSE

NEW YORK

Library of Congress Cataloging-in-Publication Data
Rossellini, Isabella.
Some of me / Isabella Rossellini.
p.   cm.
ISBN 0-679-45252-4
1. Rossellini, Isabella.   2. Motion picture actors and actresses—
United States—Biography.   3. Models (Persons)—United States—
Biography.   I. Title.
PN2287.R7584A3   1997   791.43'028'092—dc20
[B]   96-35809
Random House website address: http://www.randomhouse.com/
Printed in the United States of America on acid-free paper
24689753

Book design by J. K. Lambert

To my ghosts

ACKNOWLEDGMENTS

I would like to thank Annie Armstrong, my assistant, for typing and retyping my manuscript and correcting my numerous spelling mistakes without ever making me feel embarrassed about my ignorance. She also found the title for this book: "Your first book can be *Some of Me,* followed by *More of Me* and, on your deathbed, *All of Me,* when you can finally tell it all without lying." I took her advice.

Bob Gottlieb—his commitment to being my editor gave this project a weight and importance it wouldn't otherwise have had. Thanks to him, I was taken seriously, even by myself. When my attorneys, Robert Levine and Loren Plotkin, suggested I write a book, I thought, "If Bob Gottlieb thinks it's okay, maybe I'll do it."

I'd like to thank—and apologize to—my family and friends, who have to put up again (and this time publicly) with my exaggerations and lies. I also apologize, of course, to my ghosts and to my children, who have to understand that it is not all right to lie and that I should not be doing it.

I am grateful to Oberto Gili for offering his time and work in photographing my home and personal objects, and to Bruce White, and to all the photographers—Eve Arnold, Richard Avedon, Arthur Elgort, Hans Feurer, Brigitte Lacombe, Annie Leibovitz, Alex Liberman, Peter Lindbergh, Steven Meisel, Sheila Metzner, Helmut Newton, Pierluigi Praturlon, Paolo Roversi, David (Chim) Seymour, and Bruce Weber—for allowing me to show the work we have done together, of which I am so proud.

I'm also most appreciative for the assistance of Fulvia Farolfi and Didier Malige.

At Random House I'd like to thank Harry Evans, Ann Godoff, J. K. Lambert, Kathy Rosenbloom, Benjamin Dreyer, and Andy Carpenter for guiding me through this process.

SOME OF ME

THIS BOOK

"Aren't you the daughter of film actress Ingrid Bergman?" Yes, I am.

"Your father, the great filmmaker Roberto Rossellini, was a genius." Maybe.

"Aren't you the actress in *Blue Velvet*? That film blew my mind."

"You're the Lancôme girl. I love your ads!"

"I love your mom." Or "My mom loves you."

"You're a mom, remember?"

These are the ways I'm mostly identified, and I understand
my demographics according to them. The "Ingrid-Bergman's-
daughter group" is generally people over sixty, middle class or
aspiring to it. The "Roberto-Rossellini's-daughter group" is film
buffs, scholars, intellectuals, mostly European or lovers of European culture. The *Blue Velvet* group" is generally not older
than thirty-five, attended college, and is of liberal tendencies.
The "Lancôme-girl group" is women between twenty-five and
sixty; that's when it generally switches to "I love your mom." "My
mom loves you" instead is from very young teenagers—mostly
daughters of the group that identifies me as the "Lancôme girl,"

though "girl" I am no longer and I lost my job because of it. "You're a mom"—that's who I am for Elettra and Roberto, my children.

Once I am identified, I seem to provoke curiosity that ranges from "How does it feel to be the daughter of famous parents?" to "Does the stuff you promote—those creams—really make you look younger?" or "You fall in love with film directors—Martin Scorsese, David Lynch—who knows who'll be next? Do you have a 'father' problem?" to "Why did you adopt? Can't you just marry and have babies like the rest of the world?" These are questions I would really like to answer in this book because I'm always asked them but don't really know what to say.

"How do you keep your private life separate from your professional life?" That one I know the answer to. I don't. I don't separate anything, and I don't separate from anybody. Everything blurs and mixes together. Separating my private life from my professional life I cannot do. I can't even separate my two careers, modeling and acting; they are the same for me. I can't separate adulthood from childhood, and worse, life from death.

"What is beauty? You think of yourself as a beauty?" I don't know. A feeling of great embarrassment assaults me every time I'm asked that, and I'm afraid of giving the wrong answer. "Yes"—too pretentious. "No"—too modest after all the fanfare about my looks.

"What about style? What does it mean for you?" I truly never think about it. The way my style comes to me—and some people think I have a great deal of style—is that I do what I like. If I had to write a book about style, I could write it in one sentence: "Do what you like."

But let's start this book with answering the questions about my parents, Ingrid Bergman and Roberto Rossellini. Let me write something about them right away so we can get it over with. I know there's a lot of curiosity about them, and I have learned that before I'm allowed to speak about anything else or move on to any other subject, I first have to satisfy that curiosity, otherwise people aren't really listening to me but just anxiously waiting for me to get to my parents. Let me warn you, though: don't expect confessions, revelations, not even the truth. It's a habit of mine to embellish and color events until I lose sight of what really happened. Even when I was a child my grandmother always had to ask me, *"Verità o fantasia?"*—"Truth or fantasy?" If you want to eliminate my grandmother's kindness and put it more bluntly, I lie. I always did.

ABOUT MY FAMILY

"What is it like to be the child of famous people?" is the question I'm asked most frequently about my parents. The answer to this question is really: "I haven't been the daughter of anyone else, so I have no terms of comparison." But I know it's an unsatisfactory answer. Let me make it longer than that.

You see, my parents are "myths," and that means that everybody has a highly personal idea of who they are. Obviously it's a projection, a fantasy, but it's very vivid in people's minds. What I say about them can be different from that fantasy, and people don't like that. Of course, I can say what everyone else says, just repeat what people want to hear, which I've done, don't worry. . . . I have indeed, and gained a lot of sympathy and approval from it, and I enjoy that. I do like to be liked. But truly it is hard for me to understand the collective unconscious about

My mom, my dad, my brother Roberto, my twin sister, Ingrid, and me

Mom and Dad. In school I would always ask my classmates, "Is my mom as famous as Joan Crawford? How about compared to Greta Garbo?" I needed a kind of barometer. It was hard for me to understand the degree of her fame.

My daughter has had the same problem with me that I had with my parents. For fourteen years, my photo appeared in the massive advertising campaign of Lancôme cosmetics around the world. When Elettra was born, my photo was already there in magazines and on TV, billboards, and posters. When she was in kindergarten, the teacher instructed the children what to do in case they got lost: look for a policeman, learn your address and phone number by heart, that kind of thing. Then she proceeded to interrogate the kids. My daughter was asked, "What would you do if you got lost in an airport?" Elettra answered, "I'd look for my mamma's poster and wait underneath it for help." She thought that ads were just photos of mothers that were plastered around airports, streets, freeways, in case kids got lost and needed help.

My nephew Alessandro suffered from the same kind of problem. He had a teddy bear he believed was a male, his son, and he named him "Ingrid Bergman." Alessandro kept hearing this name pronounced with some kind of mystic aura, which he never connected with the person he called "Grandma."

I named my daughter "Elettra Ingrid" because I loved my mom and dad. Elettra is the name of my father's mother, the only grandparent I knew, since the others were dead when I was born.

"How could you call your daughter Elettra? It's the opposite of the Oedipus complex, it's about penis envy. The Elettra complex is exaggerated love for the father, tied to hating the mother.

In the Greek drama, Elettra goads her brother, Orestes, to kill their mother, Clytemnestra, because Clytemnestra and her lover had killed their father, Agamemnon."

Well, I didn't know all that, but guess what . . . it's an incredible coincidence, or, if you prefer, one of these Freudian things where your unconscious knows better than you do. I had the Elettra complex, I may still have it. I loved my dad exaggeratedly. I never wanted to kill my mother, I loved her, but as a child I was definitely my dad's girl.

When I had my son, I called him "Roberto" and gave him the middle name "Robin" for my love of animals and because I don't want anyone to nickname him or call him anything that won't at least sound like my dad's name.

"Poor child, he should have his own name. Roberto Rossellini! It's like being called 'Alfred Hitchcock' or 'Greta Garbo.' He will always feel the weight of this name, and people will make fun of him."

People! People! People! What can they say? What can they do? "Fuck them," recommends my friend Gary Oldman, the actor and now director. "Who are 'they,' anyway?" Gary follows the question with a little pause, as if waiting for me to answer. But inevitably he feeds me the answer he hopes will cure my ever-present impulse to please, which he considers deplorable. "Fuck them. Remember, this is the shortest prayer in the world: Fuck them!"

I was familiar with "Fuck it" from years ago, when I was married to Martin Scorsese. He would wake up saying it over and over in fast succession. "What's the matter with you?" I would ask. "The day hasn't yet started, nothing's gone wrong, so why start cursing?" But it wasn't cursing. I understood that later, when I acquired a little more wisdom. "Fuck it" was a necessary pronouncement, like a mantra. It helped Martin gather energy to get out of bed and face a new day.

With a "Fuck them" and a "Fuck it," I gave my children family names. If I hadn't, I would have succumbed to my parents' fame instead of to my love for them. It would have been like giving fame control over my choices, and I don't want that. To me, my dad is my dad, first and above all, and my mother is my mother. If I were to have another child and it was a girl, she would be called Ingrid, and that's that. "Why don't you simply give your children names you like?" For a boy I like Rocco, Morgan, Sterling; for a girl Maria, Francesca, Anjelica . . . but "like" is an unsteady thing with me. What I like today I may not like tomorrow, so I decided to stick to tradition.

Tradition calls for children to have their grandparents' names, especially the ones who are dead. It's all that is left of them—memory. And neither of my children knew my parents; all they'll have is what you people have: the *Casablanca*s, the *Open City*s, the *Notorious*es, the scholarly books on their work and the unauthorized biographies, the occasional photos in magazines for special editions such as "The 50th Year of *Life*" or "The Hollywood Legends," and, because of the big scandal their love provoked in the fifties, in the collections of "The Biggest Loves of the Century" with Liz Taylor and Richard Burton, Wallis Simpson and Edward VIII, and the prince and princess of Wales.

My children also get glimpses of my mom in TV promotions for film programs. She makes it into almost all of them: TNT, American Movie Classics, the Independent Channel. At home when we hear the TV jingle for movies (we recognize it because it always has that soaring, heartbreaking music), we stop and check if she's in it. Most of the time she is. When she isn't, I grimace at the TV set as if to say, "Your loss." My children do it too, especially now that they've learned to recognize their grandmother. You know, in black and white with those hairdos and that dramatic lighting, all stars can look a bit the same.

Both my parents are in just about every encyclopedia. I check, you know. When my father's entry emphasizes his marriage to my mother, I know it's an American edition. When the emphasis is on his revolutionary and innovative work as a filmmaker, I know it's a European edition. In Chinese encyclopedias my mother isn't mentioned at all and my father's work is described as "nonbourgeois telling true stories about the proletariat." That's the Communist edition. There are many ways to love my parents. Then there is my way, which is mine only.

SOMETHING ABOUT MY DAD

My father was a Jewish mother. But let me add something about him I can say only now that he's dead. He was fat. In my family, this fact was always diplomatically diminished with "He's not fat, he's robust."

When we were children (there were seven of us), one of our favorite games was throwing ourselves onto Daddy's body. Lying on his side, he pretended to be the sow and we were the piglets. My daddy always regretted not being able to nurse us in real life, though for a long time I believed he was pregnant. I arrived at this conviction because I misunderstood my baby-sitter's confusing explanations of childbirth and because of the scandalous

articles about my family in tabloid newspapers. The tabloids talked about my parents' divorce and of a mysterious, exotic woman (only later on did I realize they were just talking about my stepmother, Sonali, who is considered exotic, I guess, because she comes from New Delhi) and of "extramatrimonial" children. This word, "extramatrimonial," was just like "extraterrestrial," and I gathered that this was maybe what we were and why we deserved so much attention from the press.

"Extramatrimonial" also made me think of supernatural phenomena, and my father had this big belly, just like a woman nine months pregnant. I liked him just as he was, fat or robust, whatever one wants to call it. People who talked to him about dieting irritated me—I didn't want less of him. He was soft to embrace, and there was a lot of him. I wanted him a lot, and I wanted all of him.

One of Dad's biggest passions was driving—in his youth he had been a racer for Ferrari. Often, he would load us all up in his car and drive through Italy's little villages and cities. He would drive fast, with the horn down, klaxoning all the way, whistling Neapolitan songs and telling us fantastic stories that inflamed my imagination. I remember his hands, covered with liver spots, grabbing the wheel like a champion car racer, tightly and strongly. I thought his hands were beautiful. Years later, when I saw a few liver spots appearing on my own hands, I went proudly to show them to an art director—something else to photograph, I thought. He was horrified.

At Sunday lunch, when the family was united around the table, my brother Gil would play the sound of racing-car engines he had taped at Maranello, the Ferrari headquarters he frequently visited. My father loved to hear all that bustle. I did not. To show the depth of my disgust, I didn't rush to get my driver's

license at eighteen. Missing it then, I missed it forever. I still don't know how to drive.

It was my brother Roberto who, slapping my father in the face, convinced him to give up racing cars—he was only three years old when he took this matter into his hands. He had witnessed my mom's agony at waiting for Dad to come home safely.

But most of all, I remember my dad in bed—he loved being in bed. He stayed in bed all day long; he didn't want to waste energy. You can call him lazy, but I still connect physical laziness to the kind of spiritual and intellectual wisdom my father possessed. If someone strikes me as lazy, my first reaction is to listen carefully to what he says for some possible great truth. As an adult, I like a "lazy body" look in bed. An athletic body with muscles I could never love. In bed my dad kept books, magazines, newspapers of all kinds. He read a lot and talked on the phone. He had meetings with collaborators, students, and producers, all from his bed. Even his film-editing table was placed next to his bed.

SOMETHING ABOUT MY MOTHER

My mother, instead, had great physical energy. She walked *fast*, and when she wasn't acting she cleaned and organized the house me-tic-u-lous-ly. She loved acting more than cleaning; she loved acting most and above all. It took me some time and some doing not to feel hurt by this. I wanted to come first. When asked what was the most important thing in her life, she would flush and get all nervous, but she couldn't lie or be diplomatic, she had to say "Acting," though I know that for our sake she wished she could have answered "Family." Once in her dressing room at a theater she said, "If for whatever reason I couldn't act, I'd still do something in the theater. I'd be a dresser, anything, but I want to be in a theater." It was the only time I heard her state an alternative to acting if acting wasn't going to happen. But of course it happened and in so big a way that she didn't have to spend much time thinking of alternatives, the solution "a dresser" suggesting how little she thought about her other options.

"I want to die with my boots on"—that was what really preoccupied her: how to work right up to the end of her life. She would worry about losing her health, her energy, and consequently acting. At the question "What's the first requirement for an actress?" she would inevitably answer, "Good health." At the

My MOTHER, MY TWIN SISTER, INGRID, AND ME

question "What's the requirement for a happy life?" she would answer, "Good health and short memory." She stole this last answer from Claudette Colbert, and when she finally met Claudette, Mother apologized for the theft. "Don't worry," Claudette said. "I got it from . . ." I don't remember any longer who it was—George Bernard Shaw or Virginia Woolf or someone on that level. See, that's my problem—I remember, but not too well, which may be good for my happiness, if Mother is right, but makes storytelling hard. When I forget, I rely on fantasy. I round out my stories with inventions. That's another way I end up lying, which I've already confessed to. I lie. Indeed I do.

Second to acting, Mother loved cleaning, which is not to say she loved even that above me. I'm sure she loved me more than cleaning, but what made her happiest was combining the two. We cleaned together.

"Never leave a room empty-handed," she would often say to me, meaning that there's always a glass in the living room that needs to be taken to the kitchen sink, a magazine in the bedroom that has to be returned to the living room, and so on. She taught me how to be orderly and how to clean house efficiently.

I excelled at doing *"la vaisselle,"* as we referred to it, always using the French word. (In English there is no single word, you have to combine two: "dish-washing.") Unfortunately, this skill my mother passed on to me is not of great use today, because most people have a dishwashing machine. But let me write about it anyway, because she perfected *la vaisselle* to a science.

Take a party, for example. It's over, everybody's leaving. First thing you do is eliminate everything that smells: ashtrays, wine bottles, food. If it smells bad, you aren't going to stay around long enough to do the job, so create an environment you can survive in. Plan to do the glasses last, when everything else is clean. You need lots of big surfaces to let them dry, because you don't dry glasses with the dish towel. Glasses will never look as good as when they're rinsed in the hottest water and left upside down to dry—the hot water evaporates quickly, leaving them spotless. Wash the pots and pans first; better yet, wash them immediately after cooking, not after the party. Do the rest of *la vaisselle* in this order: plates first, silver second, serving plates and bowls last. You have to have two sinks or at least a sink and a plastic bucket. You clean and rinse dishes in separate containers. Don't try to do it all at once, the way many people do. (That really upset my mother—she thought it was one of those ridiculous mistakes that are perpetuated for no reason, the most despicable kind of mistake because it's stupid.) Use a brush, not a sponge, to wash with—the kind with a straight handle and a round tip is best. I still get mine in Sweden, where my mother bought hers. They are just perfect, you can do the glasses with one stroke.

When my stepfather, Lars, bought the Théâtre de Montparnasse in Paris, my mother rushed in to clean it. "That poor housekeeper," she told me, referring to the lady who generally did that job, "she had to work with the dirtiest rag and the most plucked-out broom. How can she do a good job? I told Lars, 'Make sure she has what she needs. You cannot clean with an unclean rag or sponge; that just lets you spread dirt around—push it a little bit here, a little bit there. It doesn't help eliminate it.'"

I am still on the lookout today for the best sponges, best vacuum cleaner, best rags. When I come to New York, where I live, from Italy, I always pack one of those special wicker things that beats the dust out. (See my drawing.)

When the weather is good, I beat my carpets and pillows out

the window. You should see how much dust comes out! The vacuum can't do it, it just cleans superficially. You can get great satisfaction at seeing all that dirt fly out.

I love cleaning. For both Mother and me, cleaning and organizing are soothing, though because it feels good we may do too much of it. It can get obsessive, and we have to watch out for that. My mother even had to go to a doctor—she couldn't stop cleaning, and everything got a little out of hand. The doctor diagnosed that she was allergic to dust, which is why she felt so strongly about getting rid of it, but I know that wasn't it. She was seeking that "high" that cleaning gives. I know what it feels like; I'm always on the lookout for dust in secret places where I haven't looked before to see if any has landed there. If I see it, I can't stop thinking about it until I get rid of it. Dust brings out the hunting instinct in me, and I know I got that from Mamma.

My mother was also terribly practical, and I am too. This bonded us—we actually worship practicality. We consider it one of the greatest qualities in people. We give it the same status as intelligence. We prefer it to erudition, which often just intimidates us—but we agreed that we like humor most and above all.

Practicality and down-to-earthness are what made my mother advise me to learn English and typing. "If you know both well, you will always find a job." She so tormented me with this ultimate solution to life that I couldn't learn either one until later in life, when my sense of rebellion was satiated. My punishment for this youthful and silly rebellion is that now I speak English with an accent. It has to do with the brain—neurological synapses, development of who knows what—but after age thirteen or fourteen, you can still learn a foreign language but apparently you get stuck with an accent. Do you know what a handicap that is, especially for an actress? Stupid me! As for typing, I don't know how to do it well, but seeing what poor English has done to me, I often promise myself to pick it up. It's on the list of my New Year's resolutions year after year—no longer typing but learning how to work the computer. If my mother were alive today, she would "upscale" her solution for life problems from typing to computing. No doubt about it.

My mother was not a cynic, not at all, but her practicality could manifest itself in ways that might be interpreted as such. Practicality carried to the extreme could result in cynicism. For example, before dying, Mother organized all her things. She left three dresses wrapped in plastic, each with a little paper note attached by a safety pin. The notes were meant for us, her children, and posterity, because although she was modest she also understood her importance. With a dry matter-of-factness the notes announced: "First marriage," "Second marriage," "Third marriage."

Another example of practicality carried to an extreme was the two windows in her living room, which Mother decided were the perfect places for the framed photos of her friends. Into one window went all those who were still alive, in the other all who were dead. When a friend died, Mother would move the framed picture over to the appropriate window. But as she grew older, the rate of those who died greatly exceeded the number of newly acquired friends. The windows had the distinction of being orderly, no doubt about that, but with time they became the most ghoulish and depressing sight in the house.

This house was the one where she lived with her last husband, Lars, on the outskirts of Paris. My dad lived on the outskirts of Rome with Sonali and their offspring, Gil and Raffaella. The three children from Ingrid and Roberto's marriage—who were called Ingrid and Roberto and me, Isabella (whose name was chosen from among a list of names starting with "I," as in Ingrid)—lived in a different apartment from my father and mother. We lived with Argenide, the housekeeper, her son, Orlando, and a never-ending flow of baby-sitters coming from the best baby-sitting services all over the world—English nannies, Swiss nannies, German nannies—none of whom stayed with us longer than a few months. Our "children's apartment," as it was called, was organized to suit our needs. Mother's practicality dictated the elimination of all grown-up furniture. Into this category fell such things as antiques, crystal, silver, sofas, carpets. The living room, for instance, had only a long dance barre along the wall, a punching bag, and a Ping-Pong table. For love of practicality, Mother, without hesitation or aesthetic consideration, shortened all the curtains around the apartment to a strange midlength, out of the reach of the dogs' lifted legs. One of our dogs—actually my personal one, Nando—persisted in peeing on everything in the house. He was male, you see, and he had to mark his territory.

As unaesthetic as these curtains were, they became my definition of true elegance, and my answer to the question "What is style for you?" comes, yes, from my mother, but not from her conventional and very admired ladylike ways, but from her originality. True elegance is for me the manifestation of an independent mind. Mother's sense of practicality dictated that all useless things are a waste, so much so that to this day, I cannot wear a shirt that has a fake pocket or any garment with a button that's just there to decorate but doesn't close anything. Everything for me has to have a purpose.

EVERYTHING HAS
TO HAVE A PURPOSE

Objects that decorate my house have a history; they aren't just there to look pretty. There's the carved Neapolitan market that's there to make my heart a little melancholy about a city I love but see so seldom.

There are the stones around my sink, all from places meaningful to me. One is from Dannholmen, the little Swedish island my mother used for summer holidays, where she wanted her ashes to be scattered. There's the volcanic black one from Stromboli, where my parents fell in love and made the film with that title. There's the San Pietrino from Rome, the cobblestone referred to as the "little San Pietro" that makes me think of my native city and the 1968 movement during which we used to throw such stones at the police. There are the ones picked up by my aunt, Zia Marcella, from the beach at Santa Marinella, where we had our summerhouse, which she used to make a soap dish. There are stones from the holy Ganges to make me think of my Indian relatives.

Next to my bed there are Madonnas, Christs, Vishnus, crucifixes, devils, burning souls, horns, and a Buddha—all there together just in case one works better than the others, and to celebrate coexistence.

There's the "bee board" that David Lynch made for me, to humor my love for animals, and

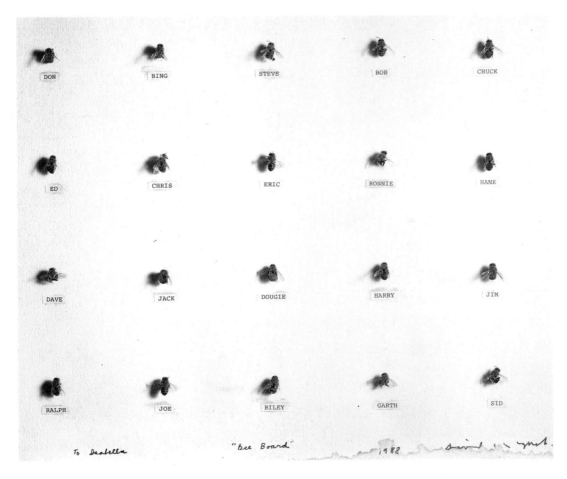

DON   BING   STEVE   BOB   CHUCK

ED   CHRIS   ERIC   RONNIE   HANK

DAVE   JACK   DOUGIE   HARRY   JIM

RALPH   JOE   RILEY   GARTH   SID

To Isabella   "Bee Board"   1988

his "chicken kit" with instructions on how to put back together
a butchered chicken like those you buy at the supermarket.

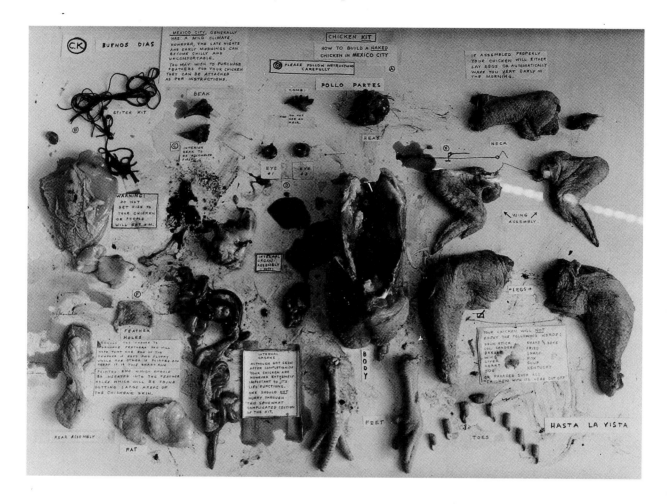

Framed on the wall are the stamps the Italian government is-
sued with an image from the film *Open City,* which my dad directed. They made me feel we had reached a pinnacle of fame.
My dad even got a street named after him.

My mother's four Oscars are now safely kept in the archive at
Wesleyan University in Connecticut, but on my desk, to coun-
terbalance all this success and remind me of another aspect of

Ingrid Bergman är på
Island och spelar in
amerikansk TV-serie
om **Indira Gandhi.**
– Hennes äktenskap
sprack på grund av kar-
riären, hon hade skuld-
känslor för försumma-
de barn – precis som
jag.
Vem kan identifiera sig
med henne om inte jag,
säger Ingrid anspråks-
löst. *FEMINA*
28 sept 198¹ 69

fame, I keep a little article my mother framed. It was to remind herself not to get upset with the press. The newspaper wrote, clearly not thinking for a moment that it must have gotten some wrong information, "Ingrid Bergman to make a film about Indira Gandhi in Iceland." She was actually making a film about Golda Meir in Israel. As my mother put it, "They just got the 'I' of 'Iceland' and 'Israel' and the 'G' of 'Golda' and 'Gandhi' right."

DEATH

My father died, and four years later my mother died too. Dad died suddenly of a heart attack. As my mother said in a letter to Jean and Dido Renoir, "He died fast, just like he drove his Ferrari." My mother died slowly of cancer, but "with her boots on" as she had wished. It was, in fact, my sister Pia who had to accept on her behalf the Emmy Award she received posthumously for her portrayal of Golda Meir.

When Daddy died, I couldn't imagine life without him. I got angry at *The New York Times* for calling him "the late Roberto Rossellini." "How dare they," I grumbled, "remember him for not being punctual after all he has done for the cinema," until it was explained to me that this was another of my mistakes in English like "revolting doors" instead of "revolving doors," "the escaped goat" for "scapegoat," and the order I can never remember for the famous trio of "Dick, Tom, and Harry" or "Tom, Dick, and Harry" or "Harry, Dick, and Tom."

At the time my father died, I was too young to know the power of fantasies, dreams, and memories. If I had to divide my own life the way history is divided into B.C. and A.D., I would choose as the dividing line June 3, 1977.

I was born on June 18, 1952. ☽ —that's the symbol in my calendar for my or anyone else's birthday I celebrate. The cross, like this—✝ —is my symbol for remembering the anniversary of anyone's death I commemorate. I don't know yet where my own ✝ will be placed, but it will be on one of those 365 days. When I look at a calendar, this thought gives me a chill down my spine.

I keep a ✝ on April 13 for my sister-in-law Lisa, who died of a death so cruel I hadn't known it existed. I have a ✝ on July 4 for Zia Marcella, my favorite aunt, who had the longest nose I've ever seen. If she had been an American, it would have been cropped by a plastic surgeon, but, since she was Italian and born before World War I, it was thought of as a sign of distinction. My family, in fact, has no aristocratic title, but that long nose seemed a revelation of some kind of genetic, even if illegitimate, connection to blue blood.

I have a ✝ for my cousin Franco, who died of "a touch of AIDS," as he put it. This definition, which conjures up an image of restraint, seemed to him the appropriately elegant way to have anything—a showcase of the well-mannered Rossellinian manner that could be another proof of our aristocracy. A drop of champagne, a pinch of sugar, a shadow of cocaine. Yet there was nothing in Franco's life that was a drop, a shadow, a pinch. Everything was excessive, immoderate, and extremely eccentric.

He managed to die on June 3, the same day as my dad but in a different year. I believe he did it on purpose, to prove to me once and for all that he was the one who resembled Father, the great patriarch, the most. Not my eldest brother, Renzo; not my brother Roberto, who carried the magical name; not my brother Gil, whom Father probably favored above all of us; not me, who everybody in the family knew aspired to the title, in spite of the fact that I'm female.

I have a † on March 23 for our housekeeper, Argenide, whom my mother referred to as "Algida," Italy's most famous brand of ice cream, because she couldn't seem to learn her difficult name. "Without Algida I wouldn't be an actress. With four children to look after, I needed her more than I needed an agent to allow me to have the career I've had," she used to say. Argenide was like a second mother to me. She died of breast cancer just like Mamma and right after her. This may be proof that they were mysteriously and supernaturally connected, as I always suspected.

My mother has a ☙ and a † on the same date, August 29. She died on her sixty-sixth birthday. Everyone found that strange and read supernatural meanings into it. I believe it was yet another expression of her very orderly, neat, Swedish way.

These are what I call *"i miei morti"*—"my dead ones." I talk to them, feel their presence. I'm not really religious, though I was brought up Catholic. I can be called . . . I

My WALL OF ANCESTORS PHOTOGRAPHS

forget the name . . . you know, the religion that worships ancestors; that, plus a touch of paganism too. I keep on a wall the photos of all the ancestors I've been able to find. I was able to gather seven generations.

At first, I hung all these photos in my daughter's bedroom. When she realized that these people were dead (except for her paternal grandparents, Flo and Fred; her dad, Jonathan; and me, her mom), she stopped sleeping and refused to enter that ghost room. I had to transfer the ancestors to the hallway, where they share space with my pets. That's where my cats and dogs are supposed to sleep, but their determination to sneak into one of our beds has always been greater than mine, which is for them to stay out there with the ghosts.

When Mother died, my sisters and brother collected her things so that they could close up and sell the apartment in London. I stayed in New York, very pregnant with Elettra and unable to travel. Pia called me. "You know the photos Mother keeps next to her bed?" she asked me. Of course I knew—there were the four of us children; Lars, her husband (though they were divorced); my cousin Fiorella (Zia Marcella's daughter), whom Mother had grown to love as her fifth child; Mother's mother, Friedel, who had died when Mamma was only two; her dad, Justus, who had died when she was twelve; and her Aunt Ellen, who had died when she was thirteen.

"Grandma's, Grandpa's, and Aunt Ellen's photos are covered with traces of Mother's lips," Pia told me. Like me and, I suspect, my twin sister Ingrid, Mother must have had secret ceremonies with her dead. She kissed those photos and whispered secrets. The connection to the beyond must have been strong, because the day she died my grandmother appeared. Mother

"To Fiorella, to remember me always. Your Ingrid"

FROM FRIEDEL'S BRIDAL BOUQUET

was in bed in her apartment. She was lucid and conscious, but dying. In the morning when she woke up, she saw her mother sitting at the dressing table. "She has come to take me," Mother announced. We knew then that by night Mother would be dead. Stop . . . stop right here . . . this is a dangerous topic. My friends always tell me, "Don't say too much about your spirituality, your dead, and what you do." Let me just say, then, that for me it's like a Gabriel García Márquez novel—you know, where the dead are just as vivid and active as those who are alive—and leave it at that.

MY GRANDMOTHER FRIEDEL'S SELF-PORTRAIT (HER GHOST APPEARED TO MY MOTHER)

ABOUT LIES

Did you notice I have already lied to you? I did. I wrote, "My mother's four Oscars are now safely kept . . ." She didn't receive four Oscars, she received three—one for *Gaslight,* one for *Anastasia,* and one for best supporting actress in *Murder on the Orient Express.* For years she was the only actress along with Katharine Hepburn to have received three Oscars until the old and already shaky Hepburn won a fourth for *On Golden Pond.* Mother was abruptly dropped from all lists of "most Oscars won by a single person." That vexed me. So I lie about it. I miss that record. I always lie anyway. It entertains me. You see, I don't *lie* lie, I just do some "coloratura." It's like filling in a coloring book with crayons, it makes my stories brighter.

I sometimes think of my coloratura and exaggerations as being even closer to truth than the truth. I'll give you an example: I was watching TV one night, and on the news I saw Paloma Picasso in the midst of an enormous crowd in a village in . . . (I can't say where; I've promised to keep the lie going). The reporter on TV explained that the government of that country had bought and restored the house where Pablo Picasso had been born, died, worked, and had his children (one of those, but I won't say which), and had turned it into a museum. Paloma was there to open it officially. A few nights later, I had dinner with her in New York—she's a friend of mine—and she asked me, "Did you see me on TV? Did I look strange? Because the government didn't buy the right house, the one connected to my father, but the one next to it. I didn't know quite what to do or if I had to say something, then I thought: It's much more 'Picasso' that way. And I enjoyed the ceremonies, which can be so boring, much more."

I agree with her. A mistake can make things so much better. It can give the human touch. It can give things a soul.

PERFECTION AND IMPERFECTION

My first husband, Martin Scorsese, the film director, knew about the power of imperfection. He even revered it. At the time, he edited his films at home and the film he was working on then was *Raging Bull*. He showed me a scene he had just put together and said, "Perfect, but it shouldn't be perfect. I like it so much, though, I can't change it." So he took a splicer and snipped a frame out of the perfect scene, though it's not enough of a gap to be perceived as a "hole" by the audience when the film is projected: "This way I know it's not *perfect* so its soul can flow through it."

I connect Martin's story, which always moves me as being the kind of wisdom that is very-old-secular-passed-on-by-the-ancestors, to Joel Schumacher's nose.

Joel is another film director, with whom I worked on a film called *Cousins*. Joel told me a story that I've adopted and give as an example when I'm asked to define style. When Joel was very young, he was assistant to Diana Vreeland, the great lady of fashion, editor in chief first of *Harper's Bazaar* and then of *Vogue*. Joel has a very long nose, so he grew a beard, thinking that a bigger chin would change the proportion of his face and his nose would look smaller as a result. Diana Vreeland told him, "You're wrong! If it's big, make it bigger. *Assume* it."

I love this definition of style. See perfection as standard and imperfection as unique, singular, original. See it as the definition of "you"—the you in *only you*—like Anna Magnani's famous bags under the eyes or Audrey Hepburn's not so famous dirty fingernails.

I saw Audrey Hepburn's dirty fingernails at a UNICEF dinner we hosted together. She was standing gripping the side of the reading stand, giving a speech. I was sitting next to the stand, waiting for my turn to speak; her hand was at my eye level. Beautiful, gracious, delicate Audrey had this strong, practical, matter-of-fact hand. I could see she had been gardening or cleaning her home, and I imagined that she didn't even shy away from a screwdriver or hammer. Worshiping practicality, as my mother taught me, I doubled my admiration for Audrey Hepburn.

The same with the other Hepburn—Katharine. She was a friend of Irene Selznick, my mother's best friend. At Irene's memorial service, I saw Katharine Hepburn for the first time and I can probably say the last time, since I've never seen her again and chances are that that brief elevator encounter is all I'll have in the way of personal contact with the illustrious star. I stepped into the elevator at the Pierre Hotel to go up to Irene's apartment, where her family and friends were gathered. Right then and there enters big, bold, strong Katharine Hepburn. Recognizing her, I lowered my eyes so as not to disturb her with my gaze. I knew that was what I was supposed to do from my mother; she always wished people would do that instead of fixing on her or talking to her or, worst of all, commenting on her looks or her latest film to whoever else happened to be in the elevator as if Mother wasn't really there in flesh and bone but was another kind of magical projection, just like the one on the silver screen they were used to seeing.

While keeping my gaze discreetly to the floor, I noticed the hem of the famous Katharine Hepburn trousers all torn to pieces, threads coming out in every direction. "The ultimate chic," I was thinking, when a loud, powerful voice blew me against the wall, my arm stretched out to the side and my hair standing straight up on my head. It asked, "Are you Ingrid's daughter?" It was Katharine Hepburn talking to me. I recognize those kinds of voices. They're actresses' voices—the clearest diction, the most commanding and authoritative delivery, and loud. My mother had a voice like that. We used to tell her she didn't need a phone, she could just have spoken to us from the other side of town and we would have heard her. She justified this habit with "I picked it up at the theater. My voice has to reach all the way to the last row." But there's more to it. Stars are made of strong stock, and that voice reveals it, no matter how sweet and vulnerable they may look on screen.

"Yes," I answered. "I am Ingrid's daughter." "The one who made *that* movie?" I don't know if it was a question or a statement—it shook up my insides because I was afraid she was referring to *Blue Velvet,* the film in which I took my clothes off—but I couldn't say anything more because before I could answer she marched out of the elevator, which had landed at Irene's floor.

Don't the wisest say, "There are no definite truths"? I hope they do, because I find it uplifting; it makes everything possible. More often I was told, "Perfection is perfection, there are standards." I cannot deny the truth of that, but it can be depressing, given that very few up there are perfect and a lot of us down here are imperfect. And depressing is not appealing—that's one definite truth. My definition of true style is the fullest, boldest expression of a self, regardless of standards: eye bags, dirty nails, shredded clothes, loudest voice.

Do you know that even the tooth my brother Roberto broke throwing a telephone at me in an argument when we were children made it? It became one of the ways of defining me as unique. This is the first ad where my real smile appeared:

My mother didn't have to cry the way she did when she saw my broken tooth, and Lancôme didn't need to get the wax from the undertakers, the one used to fix up corpses for viewing, to fill in the crack in my smile as they did for the first few years of my contract whenever I was photographed or appeared in public. At a certain point, my tooth started to be perceived as cute, a peculiarity that made me *me,* and my natural smile was revealed and appeared in advertising campaigns.

The reason I never wanted to file, fill, or cap my tooth is because I've never even had a cavity in my entire life. I need to go to the dentist only to have my teeth cleaned, and I don't want to

THE FIRST AD WHERE I DID NOT HAVE TO USE THE WAX FROM THE UNDERTAKERS TO FIX MY BROKEN TOOTH

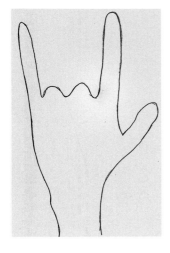

disrupt whatever is working so well in my mouth with any kind of intervention.

I always make the *corna* (horns) when I brag about something lucky that happens to me (like my teeth). I bend the two middle fingers and let the index and little finger stay up. The pagan in me makes me do it. It keeps luck from turning bad. It could help my teeth stay the way they are.

THE CORNA

I made a lot of *corna*, for example, when a glance made me perceive my house full of flowers not as festive (it was my fortieth birthday) but as funereal. I do not take these things lightly. An image that strikes my brain unexpectedly, like lightning on a clear day, is to me a clairvoyant message. I had received too many bouquets from Lancôme; they exuded some sort of guilt.

I saw my "visionary glance" justified when, six days after my birthday, Pierre Sajot, then president of Lancôme, came to Berlin, where I was filming *The Innocent* with Anthony Hopkins, Campbell Scott, and director John Schlesinger, to tell me that Lancôme had decided to replace me with another model. They were worried about my age. Since 1983, I had represented Lancôme products as their only model in an international campaign that had appeared in more countries than I can name—more than 120—and Pierre Sajot had come to Berlin to offer me the opportunity of ending our collaboration diplomatically. Lancôme was ready to announce that the decision wasn't theirs but mine, because I wanted to dedicate myself entirely to acting.

I refused. I love modeling, and I wanted to go on being available to photographers and designers who wished to work with me. Besides, I've never seen much difference between the two jobs. I also knew that this "official reason" was more of a diplomatic way out for them than for me. So I refused to take responsibility for ending our collaboration and waited to see how their decision was going to be implemented.

It started with a long procession of Lancôme employees—art directors and executives—trying to make me see reason. This trying-to-reason-with-me lasted for about two years and went along the lines of "It's going to be damaging to you if it becomes known that Lancôme let you go. It's not good for a woman to acknowledge she's middle-aged. Don't ever talk about your age, don't say anything, just graciously retire." Blah, blah, blah, blah, blah.

I don't want to bore you. I tried many times to tell this story in a funny way because that's the only way I feel it's legitimate to tell it to others, but it hasn't come out funny yet. If you cannot stand boring, just skip the next few pages.

HERE STARTS BORING

During my waning years at Lancôme, we discussed a number of solutions other than just letting me go. Lancôme felt that someone between twenty-eight and thirty-two years old is best to represent women, because that's not too old for the teenagers and not too young for the over-forties and fifties to identify with. Even my suggestion of sharing the campaign with someone younger than I was rejected. I was ready to share the work as long as I wasn't assigned only antiwrinkle creams (as has been done with older models by other companies), because that seemed a depressing idea. To me, fashion and cosmetics must help define elegance, style, and allure, and the idea of eternal youth seems so inelegant, unstylish—in fact, unintelligent. I didn't want to be confined to promoting creams that stand for something I cannot share philosophically, if I can use such a big word for it. Yet I tried to preserve our collaboration, not only because it was very lucrative but also because over so many years I had grown very attached to the company, and we had achieved some unprecedented successes that I knew would be hard to repeat.

My favorite solution was the development of a line of cosmetics and accessories around the perfume Trésor, which had become an enormous success, selling worldwide more than Chanel No. 5, which for thirty years had been the top fragrance. The other Lancôme products I had had nothing to do with—I had just modeled for them—but with Trésor it had been different. Trésor was the first product I had developed in collaboration with Lancôme, participating in the choice of the fragrance and its packaging, the photo campaign, and public relations events for which I traveled all over the world. Unfortunately, this makeup-and-accessories line that was to grow out of Trésor was killed abruptly after one and a half years of our working on it—on the day, in fact, that I believed we were to sign the final contract. I never quite understood what happened.

I was very disappointed but was told not to worry, that the two heads of the company, Lindsay Owen-Jones and Gilles Weil, had plans for me. They made dinner arrangements to announce them to me three months later, in March 1994. At the dinner, Lindsay and Gilles first suggested what I had already heard many times, namely, that I take the responsibility and officially announce my resignation as the model/spokesperson for Lancôme. In his attempt to make me understand that this was my best way out, Lindsay gave me examples from car racing. (He races cars, so he thinks that way.) He compared me with a world champion car racer who, after winning all possible trophies, retires in glory. I argued that I loved this work too much and that rather than follow the example of the car racer I would follow the one of people like Jeanne Moreau or Tina Turner or my mother, who went on working throughout their lives.

I asked if there were any signs of Lancôme selling less or losing the youth market because of me. They said no, but Lindsay explained to me that the role of an executive is to plan for the future—not the near one of two or three years but the one five or six years ahead. I argued that it would be great public relations for Lancôme to keep me on at my age; women wouldn't resent the company the way they might resent those that reach the height of absurdity by using girls in their twenties to promote antiwrinkle creams.

Lindsay dismissed my opinions. I think they even irritated him. Gilles was more understanding; he admitted that I had a point but said that it was just too marginal, valid only for a small group of people. That evening, to my great disappointment, my destiny—that is, my leaving the company—was sealed.

PHILOSOPHICALLY

I have a friend, Luciano De Crescenzo, who is a philosopher. That's what he does, strange as it may sound, for a living. In a recent letter he explained the Lancôme executives' point of view to me:

The second principle of thermodynamics states that nature can only get worse and not better. Due to entropy, beauty can become ugly, but ugly cannot become beautiful. To give you an example so that you'll understand . . .

Luciano uses my ignorance to his advantage in a kind of poor man's marketing research: if I understand what he writes, he believes, the masses will understand his books. If I don't get it, he knows they'll sell only to an intellectual elite.

. . . to give you an example so that you'll understand, an aquarium with beautiful fish can become fish soup, but a fish soup cannot become an aquarium.

Luciano may have been trying to help me by putting a philosophical gloss on my modeling problems, but this "thermodynamic principle," at least the way I understand it, is not good news when applied to middle-aged women.

GOOD NEWS FROM THE DECEASED

I think I have better news from the deceased. A few years ago I read in *The New York Times* that Lenin's body had been preserved in excellent condition by a Dr. Sergei S. Debov and was, in fact, still on view at the mausoleum in Moscow's Red Square. Every Monday and Friday for forty years, the article explained, Dr. Debov gave Lenin a checkup and a refreshing dab of embalming fluid on the hands and head. Every year and a half he was given a bath. The water in Lenin's skin was replaced with a secret embalming compound developed by Soviet scientists. "The compound has two special qualities," Dr. Debov explained. "No bacteria grow in it and, just as important, at sixteen degrees Celsius and seventy percent relative humidity it does not absorb water or evaporate. As long as we maintain these conditions, the skin remains supple."

Lenin's beautiful head is empty, though. His brain was removed the day after his death. The Bolsheviks were so certain he was a genius that an Institute of the Brain was founded to study it, and in subsequent years brains of other extraordinary people were also taken there, including those of Andrei Sakharov and Stalin (who shared the mausoleum with Lenin until he was removed and buried elsewhere—a political choice, nothing to do with the freshness of his corpse). "If a pathologist looked at samples of skin from Lenin and a fresh corpse under a microscope, he could not tell which is which, it is so well preserved," stated the doctor. I promptly cut the article out and sent it to Lancôme with the note "Dr. Debov may be of some help to us." But I got no response.

TALKING TO THE DEAD

What helped me overcome the disappointment of having been let go by Lancôme were my conversations with my dead. I know it's advisable not to write publicly about this, but if I omit my conversations I won't be able to truly explain how I go about making decisions.

When I lost my Lancôme contract, I started to feel my father stalking me up and down—all around me, in fact—like a ghost. I didn't want to talk to him. I could see from the way he was walking that he wanted to get into one of his arguments—you know, the ones that lead to his pronouncements, which are too rigorous, too moral, too intelligent for anybody really to live by. But since no one was ever able to shut him up when he was alive, you can imagine how hard it is now that he's dead. My mind makes him appear anywhere, anytime, when I'm awake or asleep, so I knew I had to give in and talk to him.

ISABELLA: WHAT?

FATHER: SO THE EASY WAY OF MAKING A LIVING IS GONE. WHAT DO YOU IN-
TEND TO DO? COMPLAIN ABOUT NOT EARNING LIKE A MILLIONAIRE?

ISABELLA: AS A MATTER OF FACT, I NEVER LOST MY PERSPECTIVE. I ALWAYS
KNEW I EARNED TOO MUCH FOR WHAT I DID. YOU KNOW WHAT I'VE SAID IN
INTERVIEWS: "HAVING A BIG BEAUTY CONTRACT IS THE SECOND EASIEST
WAY TO BECOME A MILLIONAIRE. THE FIRST, OBVIOUSLY, IS WINNING THE
LOTTERY." I TELL YOU, THIS ANSWER NEVER GOT THE LAUGH I EXPECTED; IT
LEFT JOURNALISTS A BIT PERPLEXED, BUT I KEPT USING IT, MOSTLY TO
PLEASE YOU; I KNEW YOU'D LIKE IT. PAYING MODELS MORE THAN NEURO-
SURGEONS IS NOT THE ONLY INJUSTICE IN THIS WORLD.

FATHER: THAT NEVER JUSTIFIED ANYBODY BEING PART OF AN INJUSTICE.

See what I mean? My father can be so rigorous, his dictums so unlivable, but whenever he gets that way my mother may turn up. She just sits next to me and gives me conspiratorial glances.

ISABELLA: IS IT SO STUPID BEING A MODEL THAT I SHOULDN'T BE SURPRISED
IF STUPIDITY RULES? BEING ASKED TO GET OUT IN MY FORTIES IS THE LOG-
ICAL CONSEQUENCE OF A WORLD RULED BY SUPERFICIALITY? ISN'T THAT
WHAT YOU'RE GOING TO TELL ME?

When I get all roused up like that, Mother intervenes.

MOTHER: DARLING, IT'S ONLY MAKEUP.

ISABELLA: MAMMA, YOU WERE TOLD YOU WERE BEAUTIFUL . . .

MOTHER: OH, YES, MANY TIMES. I FELT A BIT EMBARRASSED ABOUT IT. I NEVER KNEW WHAT TO SAY. THEN I FOUND THIS ANSWER: WHEN THEY SAID, "MISS BERGMAN, YOU LOOK SO BEAUTIFUL," I'D SAY, "ISN'T IT LUCKY?" AND FELT THAT WITH THAT RESPONSE I HAD KILLED THE SUBJECT AND WE COULD MOVE ON.

ISABELLA: AND WHEN THEY STOPPED SAYING IT AND YOU WERE JUST TOLD YOU LOOKED OLD, DID YOU REMEMBER HOW BEAUTIFUL YOU *WERE* . . .

MOTHER: I WASN'T TOLD THAT TO MY FACE, JUST BEHIND MY BACK.

ISABELLA: WHATEVER—DID IT HURT YOU? DID YOU FEEL BAD ABOUT GETTING OLDER?

MOTHER: WHAT CAN I TELL YOU? I DIDN'T PARTICULARLY LIKE IT, BUT THE ALTERNATIVE—DYING YOUNG—SEEMS A MUCH WORSE DESTINY!

ISABELLA: ISN'T IT RIDICULOUS, PAPA'S MAKING ME QUESTION MY WORK OF THE LAST TWENTY YEARS IN THE COMFORT OF A BIG BANK ACCOUNT? IT'S ALMOST OBSCENE.

MOTHER: DON'T WORRY ABOUT YOUR FATHER. HE MAKES EVERYTHING SO BIG, SO SERIOUS, SO INVOLVED. HE DOESN'T HAVE THE VAGUEST IDEA ABOUT THE PLEASURE OF PURE, LIGHT ENTERTAINMENT. WE'VE SEEN IT IN HIS FILMS—IT'S HIS GREATEST GIFT AND ORIGINALITY—BUT THE REST OF THE WORLD ENJOYS WHAT YOUR DAD GENERALLY DISMISSES AS SILLY.

FATHER: LET'S NOT START, INGRID. I LOVE HAVING FUN, BUT STUPIDITY DOES NOT ENTERTAIN ME.

That "stupidity does not entertain me" probably has a long history. I never saw my parents argue over films, but they must have. My father—rigorous, spare, correct—considered entertainment to be anything that was enlightening through deep research and total faithfulness to facts and history. My mother loved my dad's films, but also thought of entertainment in the more traditional Hollywood way: films with stars, beautiful, charming, and charismatic; fast-paced stories with appealing romantic plots, suspense, and incredible adventures. Take *Anastasia,* made by my mom in

My FATHER ZIPPING UP MOTHER'S DRESS

1956. My father must have been embarrassed by all the incorrect facts in the film—the romance, the waltz, the love-that-conquers-all-and-solves-everything, which is the underlying theme of most Hollywood movies. If my dad had shot *Anastasia,* it would have been very different. He would not have concentrated on whether she was or was not a daughter of the tsar. Rigorously sticking to the facts, he would probably have taken Anastasia's story as an example of the drama of war victims who, like herself, might have experienced shock, amnesia, exile, loss of identity. His film would have had references to the social and political events of the moment: the prelude to World War I, the Russian Revolution, Lenin, the decline of monarchy in Europe, and . . . Mother wouldn't have won the Oscar, because the film wouldn't have been considered entertaining.

ISABELLA: MAMMA, DO YOU KNOW WHAT COCO CHANEL SAID ABOUT LUXURY? "LUXURY IS THE NEED THAT ARISES AFTER THE REAL NEEDS OF LIFE ARE TAKEN CARE OF." PUTTING ON LIPSTICK OR TAKING A BUBBLE BATH IS A MOMENTARY ILLUSION THAT EVERYTHING BASIC IS TAKEN CARE OF SO YOU CAN THINK AND DO SOMETHING BEYOND NEED. YOU CAN AFFORD THE SUPERFLUOUS.

MOTHER: YES, MOVIES TOO. NOT YOURS, ROBERTO, WE AREN'T TALKING ABOUT YOU! MOVIES IN GENERAL TAKE YOU OUT OF REALITY AND DISTRACT YOU FOR A LITTLE WHILE. IT'S ALL ENTERTAINMENT—FILM, FASHION, MAKEUP, CIRCUS, AMUSEMENT PARK. I THINK IT'S A GREAT GIFT TO BE AN ENTERTAINER. I'M HAPPY TO HAVE BEEN ONE. DO YOU REMEMBER A GAME WE PLAYED WHEN YOU WERE CHILDREN, ISABELLA? WE EACH HAD TO NAME AN ANIMAL WE WANTED TO BE. IT WAS A PSYCHOLOGICAL TEST TO REVEAL WHO WE REALLY ARE. I SAID I WANTED TO BE A HORSE—THE ONE IN THE CIRCUS WITH FEATHERS ON ITS HEAD.

FATHER: IF I WERE TO BE AN ANIMAL, I WOULD WANT TO BE THAT CREATURE BELIEVED BY SOME TO HAVE EXISTED BUT WHICH HAS NEVER BEEN

FOUND—THE COMMON ANCESTOR OF APES AND MAN. IT WOULD BE FASCI-NATING AND INTRIGUING TO SEE WHAT IT LOOKED LIKE.

ISABELLA: IF I HAD TO BE AN ANIMAL, I'M AFRAID I WOULD JUST BE A SHEEP. I BELONG SO STRONGLY TO A HERD. I WANT TO STAY WITH LANCÔME, I'M ALWAYS DESPERATELY HOMESICK WHEN I TRAVEL, AND I'M STILL TALKING TO YOU AFTER YOU DIED DECADES AGO.

But my father has no sympathy for self-pity, and my mother . . . forget it! She has no patience for it either, and not much for anything else, as a matter of fact. I can hear their exasperated voices in unison ordering me, *"Come on, just snap out of it!"*

I MAY NOT LIKE MYSELF OLD, BUT I LIKE MYSELF ANCIENT

Though it may still be a challenge to find old appealing, I do love ancient, and I've got a few reasons to account for that:

1. While I was growing up, I felt privileged and superior to other children because I had a pair of shoes. That was a distinct sign of fortune in postwar, devastated, and impoverished Italy.
2. We were not allowed to play in certain fields because there could be unexploded mines from the war. The problem seemed insurmountable, and it went on and on, because apparently the unit of men in charge of finding and destroying the unexploded bombs was in fact digging them out from one field and burying them in another to perpetuate their employment.

3. I remember the cries from the street from the *arrotino*, the man who sharpened your knives and scissors on a round stone turned fast by pedaling it like a bike, and the *stracciaiolo*, who collected rags and old clothes. I saw chimney sweeps, really dirty with black soot, like characters from a Dickens novel.

4. I remember a song from the time when Italy was trying to be an empire again by colonizing Ethiopia: *"Facetta nera bella Abissina . . ."* ("Little black face, beautiful Abyssinian . . ."). I learned it from my Aunt Parrot, who always sang it. Parrots live a long time.

5. Cars were treated like horses. They were kept forever until they died, and they were given names. The most beloved one, Josephine, a Fiat 600, was handed down to everybody in the family until, too old to move, she became a generator for Maria, the seamstress on all my dad's films, whose house in the country had no electricity.

6. My family remembered Rome when it had no cars and they could still hear the sound of every fountain.

7. Zia Marcella believed that in order to finance his films, my father had sold some belongings of Giuseppe Garibaldi, the Italian hero who had fought with his guerrilla army known as the Red Shirts to unify Italy. These belongings had been kept by his friend my Great-grandpa Zeffiro, and consisted of letters thanking Zeffiro for socks and *panciere* (the Italian soft corsets worn at the waist and believed to prevent all sorts of diseases, from diarrhea and backache to flu and indigestion), a pair of Garibaldi's boots, one of which had a hole in it through which a bullet had actually wounded the hero, and some nail clippings. . . . Now, wait! This is weird. . . . How did this come about? Did Garibaldi cut his nails and send

them to Zeffiro? Did Garibaldi cut his nails and someone collected them in order to keep them as a relic and *then* sent them to Zeffiro? Joining my family in the total obsession that making films requires, I was just relieved to know that there was yet another source of money to finance Father, and I didn't question the oddness of these possessions. And now that I'd like to know, it's too late to ask, because everyone is dead.

8. The most distinct sign of my being ancient is that I was tended by a wet nurse, since my mother didn't have enough milk for me and my twin sister, Ingrid. There is a photo of us cuddled between the generous breasts of Matilde.

Most wet nurses in Italy came from the same town, Frosinone, near Naples. They would leave their own babies with some other woman who had milk so that the children could be fed. Wet nurses were paid with coral beads and silk, since money seemed too trivial a means of compensating such special service.

Years later—and I mean years later, at least thirty-five—I was in Toronto making a public appearance for Lancôme. A public appearance consists of visiting big department stores, and the visits are announced in the paper so that people can gather to see you. In this case, they were watching me, talking to me, asking for my autograph, and taking pictures. Don't ask me what the purpose of a public appearance is. They always embarrassed me—I hate being put onto a pedestal to be watched. On the one hand, it feels like being an exotic monkey in a zoo. On the other, I never felt I could live up to the expectations that had been built about me.

Anyway, I do them, and that day I was being watched and

was looking down from the pedestal, smiling at the crowd of hundreds of people, when I saw Giuseppe, my "milk brother"—Matilde's son. I hadn't seen Matilde since I was a year and a half old, and I don't think I'd ever met Giuseppe. But I knew it was he.

MATILDE, OUR WET NURSE

I called his name and asked him to come up to the podium. With tears in his eyes, he asked, "How did you recognize me?" "I don't know," I said. "I just knew." This is the only miracle I've experienced, or at least that's what I call it. This is how it felt:

Anything other than that is an elaboration I've made afterward to catch and confine "the miracle" in the boundaries of the rational.

FATHER'S MIRACLE

Although I was born in a country that has witnessed numerous miracles, I know of only one other that happened in my family. When Father died, he left no will because he didn't need to—he had no money and no possessions. The bank where he kept his account with its total of $200 informed us, though, that he had a safety-deposit box. Intrigued, we asked the bank to open it, which took some doing because there was no official will to give us the title of heirs and on top of that some of us are illegitimate. Paperwork, special permission, bureaucratic red tape—but in the end we succeeded. The safe was empty except for a dirty handkerchief in a plastic bag like those used to store food in the refrigerator. Thinking it was some sort of garbage that had gotten in there by mistake, we threw it away, disappointed at having found nothing else. I hadn't been counting on money, gold ingots, or precious stones; but maybe a letter with some suggestions on how to live my life. A few days later a revelation struck me: I knew what the handkerchief in that plastic bag had been. In fact, I can remember even now Father's bewilderment at what he recognized as the "miracle" that had happened to him.

Late in his life, and after a twenty-year relationship, Father left Sonali because he had fallen in love with Silvia. It was a passionate love that embarrassed me. I couldn't figure out what had possessed him. I had yet to fall passionately in love myself and create the same confusion in family and friends that my father did then.

One night—the night of the miracle—Silvia, after shedding many tears, came to the conclusion that instead of abandoning themselves to their love completely and without reservation, they should split up. A peculiarity of their love was that their great passion confused their minds and led them to make random decisions that were often just the opposite of what they really wanted. That obviously caused a lot of weeping, crises, and changes of heart. Reconciliations and breakups were a daily occurrence. But that specific night—the one of the miracle—the tears were not to be the same as usual. At first, Father did not even realize he had been "miracled." He placed the handkerchief he had offered Silvia to dry her eyes back into the pocket of his jacket and forgot about it. A few days later, while wearing the same suit, he found the dirty handkerchief. It should have been wrinkled and stiffened and stuck together, the way handkerchiefs get with old snot and tears when they dry up, but this one was still wet, as if Silvia had just blown her nose and dried her eyes.

Believing in divine intervention, Father questioned himself about the significance of this supernatural event. The message was too obscure to be deciphered. He must have decided then to respectfully lock the precious handkerchief in the safe at the bank and, keeping himself in readiness, wait for further signs and clarification from the Highest.

MONEY

ISABELLA: Papa, when you were alive, you always told us children to be grateful and proud that you would die poor. When you died, you were more than poor. Seven children, two hundred dollars in the bank, no belongings, no property, and a safe in the bank with just that handkerchief. And you left many debts. What is it that we should be proud of?

But Father, in all the seventy-one years he lived and the twenty he has been dead, never explained it totally. When I ask him in my imaginary conversations, he just walks away as if to say, "If you haven't got it by now, after almost a century of my repeating it, just forget it."

"Don't you see?" Daniel Toscan du Plantier, my father's friend, said to me. "Some people die before they can spend all their money. That, of course, is a conventional way of defining being rich. Whereas your father spent money as if he lived twenty years longer than he actually did. Let me explain: Some people see being in debt in a deprecatory manner. And of course, dying with debts is a definition of being poor—that's the conventional way of looking at it. But if you are an optimist— and your father was the biggest one I've ever met—having debts was just a way to live, at least financially, longer than the seventy-one years that were allotted to him. He had an absolute and disarming way of borrowing money from the banks: When they asked him to guarantee the loans, he would explain that if he had some other way to get money he wouldn't have come to the bank; he was there because he had no alternatives. And, with arguments that were so convincing and in a way that was so charming, most of the time he managed to bewilder the bank and walk off with what he needed."

His most astounding success at defeating the rules was when he managed to have my brother Roberto recognized as his son but "of mother unknown," defying all logic of nature.

When my parents had my brother, whom we call Robin or Robertino, Mother was still married to her first husband. That caused a great scandal, for under Italian law, Robertino would have automatically been the son of Petter Lindstrom, my mother's first husband—an unacceptable situation considering the animosity among them all.

MOTHER: MAKING MONEY WAS BORING FOR YOUR FATHER. HIS NEOREALIS-

TIC FILMS WERE SUCCESSFUL—HE COULD HAVE JUST MADE MORE FILMS

LIKE THEM AND MADE LOTS OF MONEY, BUT HE WASN'T INTERESTED. HE WAS A PIONEER—HE NEEDED MONEY TO EXPERIMENT—REPEATING SOMETHING BORED HIM TOO MUCH.

FATHER: DO YOU HAVE A HOME?

ISABELLA: YES.

FATHER: ARE YOU STARVING?

ISABELLA: NO.

FATHER: CAN YOU BASICALLY TAKE CARE OF YOURSELF?

ISABELLA: YES.

FATHER: THEN WHY DO YOU WORRY ABOUT MAKING MONEY? JUST DO WHAT INTERESTS YOU.

Don't mention to my dad the accumulation of money in order to become rich. Just that—"I want to be rich" as a final goal—is a life plan he would consider equal to a crime, and he would condemn you for it, if he had the power, to years in jail.

FATHER: IS IT TRUE THAT YOU'RE THINKING OF STARTING YOUR OWN COSMETICS COMPANY?

ISABELLA: YES.

FATHER: WHY?

ISABELLA: WHY NOT?

"Why not?" is one of my favorite answers, to be used on many life occasions. I feel I can disarm the toughest inquisitor with it.

FATHER: I DON'T REMEMBER THIS BEING THE DREAM OF YOUR LIFE.

ISABELLA: OF COURSE IT WASN'T MY DREAM. IT BECAME THAT AS THE CIRCUMSTANCES OF MY LIFE CHANGED.

MOTHER: BUT DO YOU KNOW ENOUGH? YOU'RE NOT THE TYPE OF WOMAN WHO IS ALWAYS THINKING ABOUT BEAUTY AND PAINTING YOUR FACE. MOST OF THE TIME YOU DON'T EVEN WEAR MAKEUP . . .

ISABELLA: BUT THAT'S TRUE ALSO OF THE LINDSAY OWEN-JONESES OF THE WORLD, AND IT'S TRUE OF YOU, MAMMA, THOUGH BEING AN ACTRESS YOU HAD TO KNOW ABOUT MAKEUP.

This answer I stole from Loren Plotkin, my attorney. After Lancôme let me go, I received many offers to go on working in the cosmetics field. The only one that had any appeal for me was to start my own business, but after some thought I concluded, "I don't know enough about makeup to have my own line."

Loren remarked:

1. "Businessmen don't have the chance to wear makeup, and they run big cosmetics companies." That struck me as very true.
2. "You know more than you think. What you don't know you can learn." That, too, made sense.
3. "You are in a unique situation, with years in modeling— fourteen alone with Lancôme—and films in Europe and America. You have to find a way to develop and evolve this potential. Don't be passive, or you'll be victimized by circumstances—like the ones that led you to be dropped by Lancôme." That, too, seemed right.

But it takes self-assurance, an incredible optimism, and maybe even a certain amount of arrogance to initiate any business and think it will work. I don't have all that. Yet with the help of a few "Why nots?"—that infallible answer that cuts short any doubt and hesitation—I went ahead and signed a deal with the Lancaster Group to develop my own line.

FATHER: I THINK YOU'RE PLANNING A COSMETICS COMPANY JUST OUT OF GREED—TO MAKE MONEY.

ISABELLA: NO. YOU'RE WRONG. THE ADVENTURE OF IT IS WHAT'S MOST TEMPTING. BUT THERE IS A PART OF THIS PROJECT THAT GROWS OUT OF A "BAD SENTIMENT." I'M ANGRY. I'M ANGRY AT THE INJUSTICE OF ELIMINATING ADULT WOMEN NOT ONLY FROM PUBLICITY CAMPAIGNS BUT FROM MANY

MAGAZINES, CATALOGUES, FASHION SHOWS. AND I THINK IT'S NOT SUCH A BAD ANGER TO HAVE, BECAUSE IN FACT IT'S FUELED MY COURAGE, WHICH NEEDED SOME BOOSTING.

PAPA, TELL ME WHY WE NEVER TALKED ABOUT MONEY, PLANS TO MAKE IT, BUSINESS MATTERS, CAREER STRATEGIES, ANYTHING OF THAT NATURE AT HOME.

WHEN ROBERTO TOLD HIS FAMOUS STORY ABOUT THE POOR BOY, YOU MUST HAVE HAD A HINT THAT WE WERE CONFUSED ABOUT MONEY.

Roberto's story—he was only four or five—was about a poor, poor, poor child. He has no money for food or clothes. He has no place to live. He decides to leave town and try his luck somewhere else, so he goes to the garage, gets into his Rolls-Royce, and drives away.

ON THE SET OF "THE MEADOW"

As for myself, I understood about money. By that I mean that I came to understand that it was necessary to make it—that it wasn't a criminal act—only after I met Frances Grill. I was twenty-seven years old when I got this essential lesson.

In my early twenties I thought about being a journalist. I didn't ask myself if this was a lucrative occupation or not, it just seemed serious, very emancipated, and in line with my family's teaching, and that was appealing.

But don't think that the imaginary conversations I had with my parents didn't interfere with that choice as well. My mother was the most fierce: "You're not going to be like these journalists asking the same stupid questions?" And while I was interviewing famous people like Woody Allen and Clint Eastwood, John Travolta and Barbra Streisand, her imaginary voice would scream in my ear, "C'mon, how can you possibly ask that?," preventing me from hearing any of their answers. It was agony.

In 1979 I did my first film, *The Meadow,* directed by the brothers Paolo and Vittorio Taviani. I did not think of myself as an actress, but I just couldn't resist accepting this offer from two of my favorite film directors. The film was a critical and commercial failure. But its commercial failure was not the major setback—the Tavianis' films had never been big box-office draws but had always been highly praised by the critics and intelligentsia. The critics called me "too green," meaning not ready to act. I felt I was the cause of this failure for Paolo and Vittorio, whom I literally worshiped. That made me decide to stop acting altogether and forever, refusing to be the cause of disaster to other directors I loved. Mother on that occasion didn't advise me either to continue acting or not but just commented, "You were right to do the film." Though the sentence was short, I knew what she meant. She was praising me for working with the talented Tavianis, knowing how scared I was of this responsibility and the confrontation with the press, which is always particularly severe for second-generation actors. And she was praising the Tavianis for always being such rigorous artists. This rigor was present in *The Meadow,* even if the film was admired less than their others and even if I *was* green.

During that time I only felt happy and at ease doing my comedy show—a kind of *Saturday Night Live* for Italian TV, with a bunch of wonderful comics like Renzo Arbore and Roberto Benigni. My mother, living in London, never saw my work, but my dad did—at least for the first year, before he died—and he en-

FOR THE PREMIERE OF "THE MEADOW", MY HUSBAND, MARTIN SCORSESE, DESIGNED THIS PENDANT, INSPIRED BY THE PHOTO AT LEFT

couraged me to pursue that career. After three years of *L'Altra Domenica,* as the show was called, its success made each of us go his own way in films, hosting other TV shows, doing concerts, and so on. Being the sheep I believe I am, I felt I'd lost my herd. Then, too, I found myself not knowing how to continue on my own.

Then modeling happened. It came to me and gave me a new path to follow, and this unplanned career has probably become my most successful one. It all started with my old friend Frances Grill, the one who, when the opportunity arose, made me understand money. She introduced me socially to Bruce Weber, who asked to photograph me. I agreed, just thinking I would buy a lot of copies of that magazine to show to my grandchildren years later. I fantasized their reaction—incredulous, I thought, just as I had been when I had seen a photo of my blind, limping grandmother, Elettra, as a young woman at the beginning of the century.

But that photo shoot led to another opportunity: Bill King. Frances asked me to go see him just as a favor to her. Frances had a modeling agency, Click, which had a successful men's division, but she wanted to expand the women's division, the real moneymaker when it comes to modeling. My going to see Bill, sent by Click, was an opportunity for Frances to start letting people know that her agency was expanding. I went in order to be kind to my friend Frances. Bill chose me for his next shoot, and I ended up on the cover of American *Vogue.*

From there my career as a model took off. Frances told me later that she had known all along I would be a success and that she had also known how to trick me into it by asking me to do her favors. For that I'll be grateful to her forever. If she had told me right away that she believed I was going to be a great success, I would have thought she was a deluded megalomaniac and I wouldn't have taken any days off from my Italian TV job to make time for Bruce and Bill. Only when I got the *Vogue* cover did Frances explain to me that I had a great opportunity before me.

She was the first one—or maybe the first one I listened to—who asked me the infamous and troublesome question, "How do you intend to make a living, a *real* living that can help you face emergencies and unexpected financial burdens?" Until then, I'd only asked myself what the interesting ways of living were and how a job could serve them. My comedy show earned me a state salary, since Italian television was then exclusively government-controlled, and Italian state salaries are notoriously low. Modeling paid incredibly well, and it didn't take me long to fall in love with the profession and be ready to do it for much less money than I was actually earning.

"Don't ever say that to anyone," Frances recommended. I kept quiet—so quiet I even pretended to forget my model vouchers, which needed to be signed by each client at the end of a day's work: "Catalogue: $5,000." "Half-day fitting: $3,500." "Runway: $15,000." The sums were astronomical. I constantly feared I might have misunderstood the amount and that if I presented my bill I'd hear "Are you nuts? Who do you think you are to earn fifteen thousand dollars a day? Do you realize you just wear one dress and then another and that's it?" Or worse: "Here's your money. Do you realize there are people who work hard and don't make that in a year?" I particularly didn't want to hear that one; my dad's voice from the beyond was enough of a torment. I just asked Frances to let me know how much I earned each month. The big income made me feel grown up.

FATHER: DID I HEAR YOU SAY THIS BIG AMOUNT "MADE ME FEEL GROWN UP"?

ISABELLA: YES, IT DID. I FINALLY FELT COMPLETELY INDEPENDENT.

FATHER: PLEASE, STOP! THIS IS RIDICULOUS. EARNING MONEY ISN'T THE MEASURE OF YOUR INDEPENDENCE.

MOTHER: BUT IT IS, ROBERTO. IT'S TRUE FOR WOMEN. MONEY IS GOOD PRECISELY BECAUSE IT CAN BUY A BIT OF INDEPENDENCE. IT CAN ALSO GET YOU THE SILVER, THE SWIMMING POOL, THE VILLA—I DID ALL THAT—BUT THEN YOU SPEND MOST OF YOUR TIME CLEANING THEM AND LOOKING AFTER THEM, AND FOR ME ALL THAT BECAME A BORE AND A WASTE OF TIME. I GOT RID OF EVERYTHING AND AT THE END I DECIDED TO LIVE NOT AS MY MONEY ALLOWED ME TO BUT AS I LIKED.

What mother liked was a two-bedroom apartment in Chelsea in London with a living room and a kitchen open to a small dining room, and most of all a spacious storage room to keep things clean and organized.

MOTHER: (CONTINUED): I ONLY LIVE LIKE A MILLIONAIRE IN RELATION TO PHONE CALLS. I WANT TO FEEL FREE TO CALL ANY OF MY FRIENDS, ANYWHERE AROUND THE WORLD, AND SPEAK TO THEM AS LONG AS I WISH. AND AIRPLANES I LIKE FIRST CLASS.

For everyday transportation, the bus and the taxi were just fine. Her silverware was reduced to a rod with knives, spoons, and forks hanging from it. (There's a photo of it to the left.)

I keep it, even if with the years it's lost some of its utensils, as a reminder of my mother's philosophy of life. The departure point of my lifestyle starts from my mother's point of view.

My mother's philosophy of life can be reduced to this rod with utensils

MY CLOSET

Let me explain, for example, how my wardrobe, based on my mother's rod with the utensils, came about. Before becoming a model, I did nothing about it. My closet consisted of T-shirts, jeans, and some old clothes my mother and my sister Pia had handed down. I also had various items I had liked when I had bought them, but when it was time to put things together nothing really went with anything else. As I had become a successful model and had to go to parties, I felt I needed to honor the industry I was working for. I wanted to find items that I would wear over and over; I didn't want my closet cluttered with clothes that would only gather dust; and most of all, I didn't want my first thought in the morning to be "What shall I wear today?" In place of my jeans and T-shirt I wanted to be able to grab a pair of pants or a skirt, a top or a sweater, and look stylish, but the effort would have to be the same as usual. I didn't want to put time into being elegant. And of course I didn't know that what I thought was a "laziness" of mine would become known as my style.

My style became clear to me the day I went to a dinner party at the home of Lindsay Owen-Jones. He's the chairman of the board, the biggest guy at L'Oréal/Cosmair, said to be the third biggest cosmetics company in the world. Lancôme is just one of this company's brands. I had to go to the bathroom, and in order to get there I had to go through his dressing room. A closet door was open. I peeped in. He had a row of gray suits, all the same or with just small nuances of darker or lighter gray, heavier or lighter textiles: wool, cotton, cashmere. There was a row of shoes: all the same! It struck me: that's what I should have, too!

I started to buy gray suits, man-cut, just like his. Then I added black, beige, and white, but white gets too dirty too easily. I tried marine blue and brown, but then I felt I had to buy brown shoes to go with those colors, so I gave them up. It makes for too many things in my closet. My closet is just a certain size, and I don't intend to make it bigger.

My shoes are all black: flat, small heel, high heel (but they hurt), boots, sandals, and a pair of sneakers (though I like my sneakers best in white). I wanted my flat shoes to be like men's shoes, and I had the hardest time finding the right model until I realized I could buy men's shoes. I don't know why it took me years to realize this simple, obvious solution, but it did.

Barbara Dente, a stylist friend of mine, scolded me for complaining about not being able to replace some black pants that the designer Zoran manufactured. "If you find something you really like, buy three or four of it." It was so logical, but I had never thought of that either.

My shirts are all white. I love Agnes B.'s—so matter-of-fact, with no frills. My favorite T-shirts are Fruit of the Loom (size 38–40, round collar, not V-neck).

I am still searching for: (1) the perfect white cotton underwear, and (2) the best socks—not too thick, not too thin, not too long, not too short, and definitely not the ones that gather on your toes when you walk fast down the street.

Bras are also a problem, but the designers Dolce & Gabbana may have solved this one for me. I never liked wearing a bra, but you see after two children . . . you know what I mean without my having to go into details that would embarrass me. I hated bras and wearing them until Dolce & Gabbana did this big, shiny, thick, black bra, the one under the blouses of the Sicilian widows, under Anna Magnani's slip in an Italian neorealistic film. This bra is a symbol of my ethnic identity. I feel that I wear a bra not because I need it but because I like the ethnic statement. My black Sicilian bra is like Angela Davis's Afro hairdo.

See, this is what great designers do—they make a sad obligation into a flair, a statement, a style.

I lied again. I wrote, "I never liked wearing a bra, but you see after two children . . ." Well, I adopted one of them, my son, so obviously I didn't breast-feed Roberto. But I love the implication "It took two children, not just one, to knock my breasts down." It's more dramatic, more emphatic, and on top of that it conjures up the idea that it took a double dose (two children) to spoil my beauty, and that satisfies my vanity.

MY MAKEUP

I never wore makeup until my Lancôme contract stated I had to wear it whenever I was out in public, so I did. Before that, I didn't even wear it on camera when I did my Italian television show. I directed and appeared in those short films—I was "the boss," so to speak. Wearing no makeup wasn't a conscious decision, I just didn't think about it. I wore none, and no one complained about it.

With Lancôme, I diligently started to wear makeup every time I had to go out, such as to opening nights, galas, fancy parties, and TV interviews, and I wore red lipstick in my everyday life. I figured red was bright and noticeable; I couldn't be accused of breach of contract with it. When I tried other, more discreet colors such as beige or pink, I feared they wouldn't be noticed, and the notorious fact that "Isabella never wears any makeup" would spread beyond my friends to the general public. Lancôme wouldn't have liked that.

To have become an icon of cosmetics is one of the things that gives the saying "Life is full of surprises" reason to exist, but I grew to love and use makeup as an instrument for my work, both modeling and acting. It is the mask that allows me to be free with my expressions and feelings.

When I played Dorothy Vallens in *Blue Velvet,* I needed my red nails even when we rehearsed on Sundays. Obviously I can't see my own face, so I didn't make myself up for rehearsal, but if my un-made-up hand, gesticulating, had flown past my eyes while I was working on one of the sadomasochistic scenes, it could have taken me right out of character. My red nails gave me enough "distance," "fantasy," "play-pretend," "be-someone-else" to help me feel it wasn't me. Embarrassment and shyness didn't assault me, as could easily have happened, and I felt free to concentrate on the daring scenes. The same thing happens with still photos. If it's a very glamorous shot, even a close-up, I prefer to be dressed up head to toe. High heels—something I hate to wear—can do something to your insides. First of all, they give you a body posture that isn't yours. It's the beginning of feeling "other." If you go with it, it grows—an attitude, a mood, a gesture. From your feet it crawls up into your face and your expression changes.

GLAMOUR AND PAPARAZZI

The maximum expression of glamour when I was a little girl was embodied for me by my sister Pia. When she turned eighteen, she came to visit us in Italy. We had never met her before. She hadn't seen Mother for eight years, because of the *scandal,* do you remember? Mother had fallen in love with Daddy, but she had still been married to Pia's dad, Petter. It seems it was the biggest thing that happened in 1949—headlines in newspapers for months, and for years afterward our house remained in a state of siege. Photographers pointed their long lenses at us all day and all night, spying on who was coming and going and through our windows hoping to catch us off guard. Soon (we could still count our ages on one hand), we, the children, had organized ourselves into a gang and declared war on the paparazzi. Armed with stones, bricks, and slings, we regularly ambushed them, to the dismay of my mother, who feared further scandal.

PIA AND MOTHER

When Pia arrived, our "enemies" tripled. She was blond and tall; she wore shorts; she looked cheerful and colorful with her red and pink nails and bright lipstick. She smiled and laughed a lot. She sat on a sofa not the way I had been told I had to sit—legs uncrossed but closed tight, hands on my knees—but comfortably, with a foot under her behind like a stork or with her legs crossed like an Indian chief or gathered up with her chin resting on her knees.

Never had I seen anything like it. Trying to emulate her, we decided that our gang should change its password to "Yes, of course." Pia said it a lot; since it was in English, we had no idea what it meant, but nothing sounded cooler.

By the time I was seven or eight I had promised myself to become a man. Nothing in the world of women seemed to me as attractive, free, and fun as the world of men. Pia was the first woman I would have liked to be. I never forgave my father for taking my brother Roberto out of school the day the Soviets announced the successful launch of the first man into orbit. My brother—not me and my sister! Father, excited and moved, had rushed to our school to announce the historical event to my brother and his classmates. He had then taken Roberto home, incapable of imagining leaving without his son. My sister and I had been left in class to finish the day's routine. We were girls. Rage and fury, that's what I felt. I was not going to be a girl.

But by the age of twelve my hormones betrayed me. Two small bumps appeared on my chest—they hurt if I squashed them, preventing me from wrestling with Orlando, the son of our housekeeper/second mother, Argenide, with the same élan as I always had. Then came my period. I was advised not to swim, not to stay in the sun, not to go near wine because it would turn to vinegar. My woman's life became more of a prison. "Now that you are a signorina"—I hated that title "miss"—"you can't play as roughly. You must sit straight and composed and beware of men." Not much else was added to that "beware of men," but a long pause accompanied by an intense look made me anticipate some kind of unspeakable horror.

It was around that time in my life that Pia came from the United States. She had decided to live in Europe with us for a while. It was perfect timing for me. When I complained about having menstrual cramps, she put me onto a horse. That was the best way to get rid of cramps, she told me. She laughed at the idea of wine turning to vinegar, and she took me swimming every day of the month.

By the time I was eighteen, with no hope left of becoming a

man, I came to live in America with Pia. She was working as a reporter for a television network, and I picked up after her, reporting from New York for my Italian comedy show. I shaped my segments by what Pia taught me.

A few years later, watching TV in Italy, I saw a strange creature on the screen: sexy, giggling, and confused. She said what she had to say while hanging from and twisting around a street pole. "She's doing you. She's trying to copy your style," a friend announced, laughing at the awkward girl. "What style? What's 'my' style?" That girl looked ridiculous to me. "Reporting from outdoors instead of from behind a desk and speaking not like a robot but just the way you do in life." Outdoors, natural, direct—I had just copied it all from Pia. I wasn't aware I had started a trend. I became a big success on TV in Italy so that I inherited the paparazzi that had followed Mother all her life. They still follow me around when I go there. Some of them are the same ones as when we were children. When I first took my own babies, both born in the United States, to meet my Italian family, the paparazzi were there photographing us. But they had tears in their eyes and they hugged and kissed and blessed my babies. We grew attached to each other. They know they bother me, following me everywhere, and my children don't want to spend their holidays in Italy because of them. "But why? You should see us as your protectors. . . . With all the kidnappings happening in Italy, as long as we keep photographing your every step nobody would dare come near you—not even for a simple *scippo*"—the famous little crime of purse snatching that is ubiquitous in Italy. In a way, they're right.

ACTING VERSUS MODELING
AND MAMMA'S ADVICE

It may be my predilection for lies that makes me want to be an actress—and a model, for that matter. To me the two jobs don't differ much.

"Well, dear, maybe you can't act. You're just using your pretty face, model that you are, to push your way into the industry in which your mother excelled."

I can hear you . . . you people, the ones Gary advised me to dismiss with the shortest prayer in the world. Let me tell you, though, that there are many similarities between the two jobs, especially with today's acting—not the kind on stage but the kind that relies on cameras for film and television. Cameras seem to have the power to photograph personality. Being charming, charismatic, and photogenic is a requirement for film stars as well as models.

There is no dialogue for a model in a still photo and no story to tell, no arc and no evolution of emotion to portray, no other actor to react to, and because of that, modeling is considered "less" than acting. But also because of that, it sometimes seems to me more mysterious. A great photo has to conjure up an entire reality in one frame without the help of the story, the dialogue, the music that creates so much atmosphere in a film.

Mamma gave me only one piece of acting advice: "Don't do anything. It's better than doing it wrong or badly. There will always be the violins to give your character the right mood."

I read somewhere in an interview about the making of *Casablanca* that she used this trick herself for her big close-up at the café, when she sees Rick for the first time after many years. She didn't know if she had to play being in love with

Rick/Humphrey Bogart or with Laszlo/Paul Henreid because the script kept being rewritten while they were shooting the film, so she decided to go blank-faced for that close-up, counting on the violins that would later be edited into the soundtrack.

Yes, I got into acting through modeling. And I applied a lot of modeling to my acting.

MODELING SKILLS
APPLIED TO ACTING

When I shot *Blue Velvet,* for example, David Lynch, the director, explained to me the feeling he wanted for the scene where I walk stark naked through a small American town. Once when he was a kid, he told me, coming home from school with his older brother, they had seen a naked woman walking down the street. The sight had not excited them, it had frightened them, and David had started to cry. My "model-trained" brain flashed me an image: the photo by Nick Ut of the girl in Vietnam walking in the street naked, skin hanging from her arms after a napalm bomb attack. That devastated, helpless, obscene, frightening look seemed to me what David wanted, and I adopted it for my scene. The ability to identify one gesture that will capture a whole mood is the model's job. It's the one thing we, as models, share with figurative painters.

I wish I'd found some other approach for the scene in *Blue Velvet;* I did not like being totally exposed, I kept worrying about what my family would think when the film came out, and I searched and searched for

Nick Ut's devastating photo was my inspiration for a scene in "Blue Velvet"

ME AS DOROTHY VALLENS IN "BLUE VELVET"

other solutions until the last minute—also because people were gathering around the set to watch the making of the film.

People came out with blankets and picnic baskets, with their grandmothers and small children. I begged the assistant director to warn them that it was going to be a tough scene, that I was going to be totally naked, but they stayed anyway. I went out and talked to them myself, but they were already in the mood of an audience and just stared at me without reacting to my plea and warning.

Time came to shoot. I apologized to them in a loud voice, knowing they were going to be upset, and concentrated on my scene. By "concentrate" I mean *just do it*. My mother, when asked "How do you remember all these lines in films and plays?" answered, "By forgetting everything else." It's true. Focusing, total concentration, is what's needed when acting, though "forgetting everything" is what my mother did anyway. It was her recipe for happiness and, I believe, the basic reason she loved acting so much.

Once we started to shoot the scene, I just beamed onto the other actors and some of David Lynch's direction. Once David called, "Cut—we have it," someone came with a robe for me to wear and my attention returned to our surroundings. Everybody had left.

The next day a notice from the police told us we would not be given any more permits to shoot in the streets of Wilmington, North Carolina.

For *Wild at Heart* I used other impressions that were stored in my brain. For my character, Perdita Durango, I used Frida Kahlo, whose paintings are a series of obsessive self-portraits.

Frida Kahlo portrayed herself as attractive and repulsive at the same time. She is beautiful and feminine, but she is hairy, a bit like an ape, with a mustache and two eyebrows that are really one big one across her forehead. This combination of attractiveness/repulsiveness fascinated me, and I told David I'd love to play a character with these qualities. A few years later he remembered what I had told him and offered me the small part of Perdita.

I used a bad blond wig that exposed black roots and a tight dress, sexy but vulgar. I changed my body posture and I added hair so that I, too, could have one eyebrow across my forehead. My Perdita, I believe, conveyed the impression of a person who

In "Wild at Heart", my character's look was inspired by Frida Kahlo

is repulsive and attractive at the same time. David and I created her character, who was in the film for just a couple of scenes, with her look and her image. Perdita is my best example of modeling skills applied to acting.

A MACHINE TO X-RAY MINDS

There is one portrait in which Frida Kahlo painted Diego Rivera, her husband, in the middle of her forehead, where the third eye is believed to be. This is how I imagine a machine to X-ray minds would photograph thoughts.

I guess if there were such a machine, we would find a lot of images we all share. Is this what is called the common unconscious? Is this what images are: a synthesis that in one frame sums up an entire event for all of us?

In my work with photographer Steven Meisel we used the archive of images that are mysteriously stored in our brains. All of Marlene Dietrich's films we condensed into one or two images—a gesture, an eyebrow, a shadow across her face. All of Anna Magnani's films we reduced to a laugh, a mass of hair, a hand over her face, which convey the world's pain. All of Sophia Loren's films we condensed into a walk I love and have copied in fashion shows, an ass trapped in a skirt and breasts she is so proud of I can read it in her eyes. We reenact, once with my cousin Franco's collaboration (in the photo with me), some memorable paparazzi shots of Italy's postwar economic boom, referred to, after Fellini's film, as "La Dolce Vita."

Here are some photos I have done with Steven, using our own mental archive:

THESE PHOTOS OF MARLENE DIETRICH INSPIRED...

... this photo of me for a Donna Karan catalog

ANNA MAGNANI: "THERE IS THE LAUGHTER THAT ONLY ITALIANS KNOW. THIS IS WHAT THE ITALIANS GAVE THE WORLD"
—DIANA VREELAND

MARIA CALLAS...

... AND ME

PAPARAZZI PHOTOS GAVE US THE IDEA FOR A DOLCE AND GABBANA CAMPAIGN
(MY COUSIN FRANCO MODELED WITH ME)

ACTING SKILLS
APPLIED TO MODELING

I applied a lot of acting skills to my modeling, too, especially when working with Richard Avedon. Dick, besides being the great maestro, the fount of fashion photography, is also a great teacher. I went to his studio a few weeks after I'd gotten my first cover of American *Vogue* with Bill King. Avedon taught me that my contribution to the photo was to act in front of the camera.

By acting, I mean that feeling that will take over, prevail upon you, crawl from deep inside outward, affecting your facial expression and your body language.

"Change your thoughts, I don't like what you're thinking," he would instruct me, and he could really *see*. Once I tested him; I disobeyed and went back to my original thought, the one he had asked me not to have. He caught me immediately: "I told you, I don't like that. Change it."

Years later, for his seventieth birthday, I sent him a video. I stood in front of the camera and just said "Dick, here—just look at me." Then I shut up and stared straight into the lens, thinking as hard as I could, "Happy Birthday, maestro!" A few days later he called, saying how much he had enjoyed my birthday wishes.

In contrast to other photographers, who work with automatic cameras and shoot many frames a minute, Avedon takes only a few frames. Once the clothing, the light, the

This photo was taken the day I understood I had to do something in front of the camera, not just stand there pretty.

makeup, and the hair are set, he just stands next to his camera, staring at the model with the most benevolent attitude, waiting to catch an interesting expression. He notices the smallest change in your face and underlines it with a smile, an "Ooh," a twitch of the mouth, which may indicate "Don't go that way" or "Beautiful" to encourage you down a path—that's how he directs.

I have developed a sixth sense for the clicks of the camera— I always know if I'm being photographed by a good photographer if I hear the clicks when I'm at the peak of my expression, when the feeling I have summoned up has totally pervaded me. A bad photographer will miss that moment because he doesn't look at you very closely. He's not into details. It was Avedon who, while endlessly adjusting a silk collar that kept collapsing instead of staying up on the back of my neck, told me, "Sorry, Isabella, be patient, remember that God is in the details." This sentence infused me with the patience to endure applying lipstick for twenty minutes. Actually, it generally takes two and a half to three hours to prepare for a photo shoot: hair, makeup, clothing, accessories.

This "God is in the details" has also helped me refrain from ridiculing and laughing at situations that may seem extreme. I haven't decided yet if I should laugh at or respect Lancôme's order to sweep the desert where we were shooting a commercial with Herb Ritts because they were afraid that the cracks in the ground might possibly suggest dry skin or wrinkles.

Avedon's photography seminar starts with a brilliant staging that is incredibly telling. The audience is in the dark and the stage is lit, the usual setup, but when Dick enters he asks for the lights to be turned onto the audience. "Now I can *see* you," he announces emphatically. "Seeing" is what photographers do better than we do.

Like any other experienced model, I never asked my agent, "Whose clothes are we photographing tomorrow?" but rather, "*Who* is photographing?" A good photographer is the number one essential element for a successful job, as a director is for a film.

I believe there were many reasons for the success of my Lancôme campaign, but one of them was that I retained in my contract the right to choose the photographers. I carefully worked only with the ones who could *see,* and the campaign stood out from others because it had warmth, feeling, and expression. We never photographed "beauty" per se. As Diana Vreeland put it, "Without emotion, there is no beauty."

You need more than beauty to be a good model, though beauty is a given in fashion and cosmetics photography. If I hadn't been beautiful—and by beauty I mean something more conventional than style: full lips, big eyes, long, slim body, and so on—they wouldn't have hired me. And that's that. Makeup artists, hairdressers, stylists, and photographers will enhance what's there to its maximum potential. As I said in my eulogy at Bill King's funeral, "I owe fifty percent of my beauty to my mother, whom I resemble, and the other fifty percent to Bill."

My responsibility as a model is not to be concerned about my beauty but to offer emotions. Any photographer can photograph a beautiful woman, but without emotion, any emotion, the image will stay remote. It will not intrigue the viewer, it will not have mystery, it will not unleash the imagination—it will be flat. Modeling, like acting, requires skill. Yet a great photo for an ad campaign or an editorial is unquestionably more the doing of a great photographer than of a model.

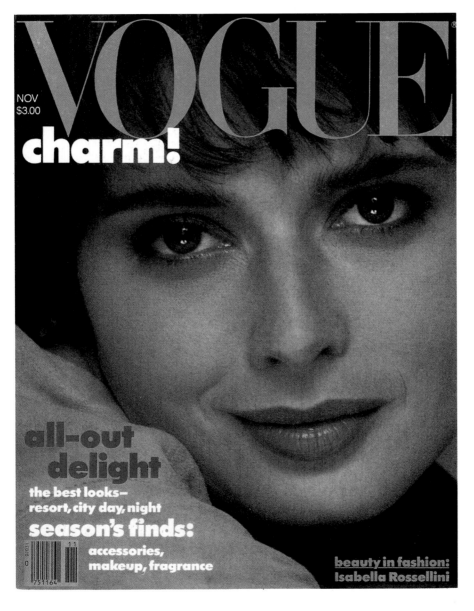

My agent tells me I have been on the covers of 300 magazines internationally. I had a total of 28 Vogue covers alone. Nine of those were by Richard Avedon.

I LIED AGAIN

I lied again—one of my coloraturas. You know, I made you believe Avedon could really read my thoughts when he thanked me for my telepathic "Happy Birthday." Well, my message to him was just one segment of a long tape of wishes from friends and acquaintances that was made for his birthday, so he knew.

But didn't having you believe he could really tell what was in my mind make you go "Oh!"? I wanted to give you that "Oh!"— that sensation of being startled. You know why? Because I bet it's similar to what I felt when Avedon, directing me, made me understand that I had to think, concentrate, and emanate something, not just stand in front of the camera. I went "Oh!" too— and became a model.

That's why lies are sometimes very good. Lying is the only technique I have for telling not the factual truth but the emotional truth. That's another reason I do it.

SHE'S BEAUTIFUL

In fashion photography, the assignment is basically always the same: to capture elegance, glamour, and appeal. The definition of these qualities by different photographers is what makes photos different, and that difference is what's interesting to me. Each one photographs my face uniquely, capturing with the camera the features he likes to emphasize. Some like the roundness of my face; some prefer a three-quarter angle to shave off my cheeks. Some like my smile, others don't. Some like to emphasize the Italian in me—dark, warm, extroverted—and some see more the Swedish in me—colder, reserved, aloof. It's interesting to see how one person (me) can be perceived so differently. It's a glimpse into the individuality of our perceptions. "Is the blue of the sky the same shade of blue if perceived by eyes other than mine?" Do you have these kinds of thoughts? I do. I guess this curiosity about different perceptions is what allows me to say, looking at a photo of myself, "She's beautiful" or "She isn't radiant enough." "She," not "I." I react to the perception of me, which is not what I sense is the real me. I guess this is the distance that allows me to have a professional attitude, a critical eye toward my work.

My "me wall" is a display of photos taken of me by different photographers. It's a display not of my vanity but of my pride at having worked with so many talents. I believe the photos reveal the photographers' personalities more than they reveal mine. Looking at my "me wall," I think of them, the photographers; I don't ecstatically contemplate my own features. Photos are such a clear revelation of each individual photographer that I can look in any fashion magazine and tell you who shot each layout without looking at the photo credits.

Cosmetic and fashion photography, despite commercial goals that inevitably push toward the standardization of an image, retain photographers' individuality. That's why I think of it as an art form—an art form in a straitjacket.

IN Bob Zemeckis's TV FILM "You, Murderer" I Spoofed my mother in "Casablanca"

SPITTING IMAGE

My mouth, the shape of my face, my jawline are my mother's. My nose, too, but only the tip of it, not the bridge; that is unique, like no one else's in the family. My eyes, my forehead, my coloring, my height are different from Mother's, but still everyone tells me, "You look like Ingrid Bergman." When I say everybody, I mean it. I catch a taxi. The driver doesn't have a clue I am her daughter, yet I hear, "I thought I was picking up Ingrid Bergman." People stop me in shops, on the subway, in the street on my way to pick up my children, to tell me, "You look like Ingrid Bergman." I can see them coming at me with that announcement—they have a specific expression I recognize. I try to look busy or in a hurry or worried or sad, but nothing works. There is still something I have to find to discourage them from stopping to say to me, "Have you ever been told you look like Ingrid Bergman?"

Whether I answer "Yes" or "No," it provokes further comment. If I respond with a "Yes," they say "You have? It's uncanny, it's extraordinary. How many people have told you this? What do you do about it? Did you ever try to contact Miss Bergman to tell her you are her clone?" If I respond with a "No," they say, "You were never told you look like Ingrid Bergman? But it can't be, because you're her clone—I swear . . ." They even stop other people in the street to enlist their support: "Don't you think she looks like Ingrid Bergman? It can't just be me. It's an uncanny resemblance. Look . . ."

The answer "I'm her daughter" should explain why I look like her and should appease their amazement, but generally it has the opposite effect. I hear all the exclamations that the "Yes" and "No" answers generate, plus I risk hearing a review of all

Mother's films: "I liked her in *that,* but she should never have made *that* . . ." Or: "She's a wonderful human being—a beautiful woman outside and inside. You're truly lucky to have her as your mother." Or the one I hate most: "I'm sorry. I'm sure you're not *only* your mother's daughter. I should stop carrying on like this about her. You want to be *you,* an individual in your own right, don't you? You are *you,* you want to be you . . ."

I went to dinner at the White House with David Lynch. It was a big dinner, for a lot of people. We stood in line to shake hands with the president and the first lady. David was ahead of me. When it was my turn, Nancy Reagan gripped my hand and didn't let go. I lost David, who was pushed forward by the line of people that moved on with the inexorability of water in a river. When I finally joined him, he asked me, "Mrs. Reagan talked to you? What did she say?" "The usual: 'You look like your mother.' " She actually said, "You indeed look like your mother," and that "indeed" made me think she had discussed this before. With whom? The president? The president of the United States and the first lady were talking about Isabella Rossellini looking like Ingrid Bergman?

Mamma and I looked at each other in the mirror and came to the same conclusion: People exaggerate. We don't look so much alike after all. But in 1979 I did this film *The Meadow,* the only film of mine Mother saw, and she said to me, "Don't you see it? We have the same gestures, expressions, voice intonation, way of walking. I didn't see it when we looked at each other's faces in the mirror, with just that one expression—a stare. Now I see what people mean!" But I didn't. I still thought people exaggerated.

Then one day I went into an antiques shop. I didn't have anything in mind to buy; I was just looking around. There were beautiful things: tables, dressers, old mirrors, lamps, chairs. I was alone in the shop with just one other customer. She looked distinguished—actually, I should say very distinguished—and you know how these upper-class people are: aloof, reserved, private. So, respectfully, whenever in my wanderings in the shop, I came too close to her I walked in the opposite direction in order to leave her alone. "She reminds me of Mother," I thought. And then—bang!—I crashed into her. I looked up at her face and . . . that lady was me! What I had seen was my reflection in the mirrors on sale in the shop. I had not recognized myself, because what I had seen was a middle-aged woman. I hadn't realized I had grown up so much. But that lady looked:

1. Slim. A relief. As a model you're always told you aren't slim enough. But I was slim, all right. And I decided I didn't need yet another diet.
2. Elegant. It took some doing, but I did indeed look elegant with my gray suit (men's cut), black coat, Paloma Picasso purse, cashmere scarf, and gloves.
3. Aristocratic, and I didn't know I had so much of that.
4. Like my mother.

People, you are right. I am sorry if I seem bored and annoyed and am abrupt with all of you who tell me that I look like Ingrid Bergman. I *do* look like Ingrid Bergman. So . . . what am I to do? What do you want from me? This admission makes me feel as if you want me to do something, but what? Or do you want me just to state something? What? As their daughter, I could have looked like my mom *or* my dad—I guess I should say I'm lucky to have taken after her. And tell me, isn't it natural to look like one's parents? Do you want me to agree with what that woman wrote in *Vogue* after they did a big profile on me: "Isabella Rossellini has the presumptuousness to think her career came from her talent rather than just her uncanny resemblance to her mother." Whoa, that hurt! Could it be only that—a resemblance? Am I just an approximation of Ingrid Bergman? A kind of impostor?

The way I see it is: being Ingrid Bergman's daughter is like being born with a great athletic body or beautiful blue eyes or great intelligence. It's an asset. But it's not the solution to your life, it's just an asset. All those assholes making comments like the one in *Vogue* are the liabilities.

There, I've said it: assholes. I can say also shit, fuck, and scumbag, as you know. You didn't expect me to swear. I'm Ingrid Bergman's daughter, and I have to behave in a ladylike way, right? When I took my mother to see Martin's *Raging Bull*, I told her, "Mamma, beware, there's a lot of swearing. Go beyond it. The film is truly a masterpiece." She looked at me and waved me off. "I know 'fuck,'" she said, and she marched on into the screening room.

THE MAKING OF . . .

When I'm stopped in the street, if I'm not told, "You look like Ingrid Bergman," I'm told, "Your sister is beautiful." People see the resemblance to my photographs, but in person, without the glamorous perfection of photography, they think my sister, not the woman standing in front of them, must be the gorgeous model.

The making of so-called bigger-than-life creatures takes some doing. I have to offer them what I have—my features and the range of my emotions—but from this foundation the photographer, stylist, makeup artist, and hairdresser will create the "bigger-than-life creature" with the added magic of filters, lifts, tucks, lighting, and retouching.

I find this process fascinating and creative, far more than just a cheat (which is what some people consider it to be). Steven Meisel photographed my Italian legs five inches longer than they are. "No wonder you like to be photographed looking so splendid, with your legs stretched longer, your belly flattened, your wrinkles brushed off in the retouching . . ." Sure I like it, but what charms me most is the reinvention of me into a fantasy.

I always wanted to assist at the aftermath of a photo session—it would be like peeping into Dr. Frankenstein's studio—but I was never allowed to. I guess photographers are afraid I'll interfere, I'll start saying, "What's wrong with my legs? You never told me you find them too short," or "I always wanted blue eyes—give me blue eyes."

The furthest I could go was to look at my photos before the retouching and editing. In the unedited rolls of film, I saw frames taken split seconds apart. There was nothing apparently different in the poses, yet one frame has life, the next is dead. I suspect that the one that has life is the one taken when I was totally immersed, overcome by some feeling I had summoned up.

During a photo session I can often tell when we've shot a good roll of film. It's when my concentration is strongest and I can anticipate the photographer's command: "We have it. Go change."

"The elusiveness of this perfection is the portrait of the mysterious longing for unobtainable dreams," explains my Ph.D.-in-medieval-literature twin sister, Ingrid. "Even Dante longed for

Beatrice—he just saw her walking across the bridge," and he went nuts, became obsessed by her. The Donna Angelicata became the symbol of all sorts of unobtainable desires.

These unobtainable desires, whatever embodiment they take —supermodels, Donna Angelicata, film stars—can backfire. Have you ever felt a greenish foam come out of your mouth with a strong wish that all the bigger-than-life creatures die? I have! It's envy, you know.

Too many dreams, too much longing, bigger-than-life qualities, all can go bad, and that is especially to be avoided in advertising campaigns. In order to lure people into buying advertised products, identification with the models, not intimidation, is the requirement. The big beauty contracts of the kind I had with Lancôme, for example, generally go to beautiful models whose beauty isn't unattainable. More brunettes get these contracts than blondes, for instance. When I started to do my public appearances for Lancôme at the department stores, I was praised because a lot of women—that is, potential buyers—came to meet me. At Elle Macpherson's public appearances for Biotherm, a lot of men came. Elle's beauty, it was explained to me, is too great. She's intimidating to women but appealing to men, who aren't, however, the right target for selling beauty creams. Not being perceived as "the fairest of them all" has its advantages.

When I signed with Lancôme, I had been a full-time model for hardly a year. My editorial work, though, was impressive. In 1982, I got four covers from the very prestigious American *Vogue* alone, including three in a row (September, October, November), which was unprecedented. I was paid $150 for each of them, but the prestige that good editorial work carries leads to big advertising campaigns. By the end of that year I was signed by Lancôme. I had also done very few publicity campaigns and catalogue work. Lancôme was particularly pleased about this "virginity" of mine but checked my professional past meticulously. A seasonal ad I had done for Revlon, which had run for three months a year before, worried them, as did an association with the Japanese house Kanebo, even though I hadn't advertised its makeup, only its textiles, and that had been four years earlier.

Frances Grill, my agent, forbade me to disclose that I had done an ad as a TV personality endorsing an Italian liqueur, Rabarbaro Zucca. Foodstuffs are considered the lowest in the class hierarchy of advertisements. Luckily for me, the ad had appeared only in Italy and Lancôme either never found out about it or else it considered Italy a small enough country not to threaten its international campaign.

MY CHINESE ADVENTURE

The liqueur I advertised was extracted from a Chinese root. As soon as diplomatic relations were restored in 1979, Rabarbaro Zucca made arrangements to film its ads in China in the remote area of Kansu, south of Mongolia, where the root grew. I was offered two tickets for the six-week trip—one for me and, it was suggested, one for my husband (then Martin) or an agent (which I didn't have at the time). Instead, I took a personal translator, Francesca Cini. I still give myself credit for this astute choice, because with Francesca's help I could speak, relate, and exchange ideas with the many Chinese I encountered. Most of them, especially in Kansu, had never seen a white person before.

I was being filmed in a Kansu field standing next to a gigantic rhubarb plant that grew as big as a tree. In front of me were horizons of hills that my mind recalls in a curious color: blue. Blue hills, all terraced. It was moving testimony to centuries of human labor in agriculture. Then I started seeing what seemed at first to be smoke pinnacles coming from those blue hills. But my mind, flashing some frames from a John Ford movie, helped me recognize that what I was seeing was not smoke but dust from galloping horses. They came toward us from every direction and crowded around the crew and me in a circle. *"Da, da,"* they kept saying—they thought we were Russian. "No, Italy. *It-a-ly,*" but they didn't seem to get it. "Pope," I said, and I made the sign of the cross, but that too seemed to get lost. "Paolo Rossi. *Ros*-si." He had just won the soccer World Cup for Italy with a sensational goal. "Rossi," they repeated. They knew. Suddenly the military police, who accompanied us, appeared. They were not pleased with that gathering.

We had traveled from Beijing to Sian and from Sian by train (I've forgotten for how long, but long). The curtains were always closed as we stopped in the stations, and our compartments were locked. We were to have no contact with the Chinese. A loudspeaker was constantly screeching. "What's it saying now, Francesca?" "It's Mao's sayings," Francesca would translate, " 'Today is cold. Remember to wear a sweater.' " Or " 'Brush your teeth and wash your hands before eating.' " Mao spoke just like anyone's grandmother. It was not the only time I came to identify and feel familiar with him. After our train trip we proceeded in military jeeps through the rural, primitive countryside to reach the rhubarb fields. We slept in military barracks on beds made of wood planks covered by thin, stiff, noisy straw mattresses. We were not allowed to leave the military compound, and we were escorted to the field to film our commercial.

When the crowd gathered, our "keepers" got upset. They took out whips and started to disperse the crowd. It was not courage that made me jump onto one of the guards and stop him. I didn't think; I just found myself awkwardly on his back, as if I were riding him. Before I could apologize, as I was ready to do, others intervened and separated us. There was a lot of commotion. We were taken back to the military barracks. I was escorted to my room and told to wait. With Francesca's help I was asked twenty minutes later if I would like to go to the village that night for a film screening. "Yes, of course," I said. Escorted by the guard, now smiling and courteous, we walked down the middle of a corridor formed by people who, as we passed, massed behind us. We arrived in a field. A white sheet had been stretched, and a sixteen-millimeter projector was ready to show a very "sugary" movie. I loved it, and I loved sharing that evening with the crowd of Chinese peasants from Kansu. Had my aggression toward the guard brought all that about? It was one of the first times I was taught a lesson I had never wanted to learn or believe: that aggressive, rude manners can work.

LANCÔME RULES

Despite what were considered flaws to my untouched image—the few ad campaigns I'd previously done—Lancôme decided to sign me as the exclusive model for its international campaign.

Our agreement required total exclusivity in cosmetic advertising, and Lancôme had the right to veto any kind of advertising campaign I might be offered in another field. My modeling for editorial work was limited as well: I was not allowed to be photographed for any stories totally dedicated to designers with competitive cosmetic lines, such as Chanel or Dior, and all the makeup I wore always had to be credited to Lancôme. I agreed to consult with Lancôme if I wanted to change my haircut. A suntan was forbidden. Minor cosmetic surgery, such as fixing my broken tooth, was considered an acceptable request, and I was not allowed to gain weight.

The contract also included a morals clause: if I were involved in a scandal, the company had the right to get rid of me. Frances at least negotiated "scandal in a major urban area," giving me some space to breathe. The only times I risked the morals clause being applied were with *Blue Velvet* and the Madonna book *Sex*. When I got pregnant, there were arguments about whether I'd breached the contract because I hadn't "maintained a slim figure" or because I'd caused a scandal by not being married. But on all these occasions we solved the problems with quarrels among us but no legal proceedings.

In 1992 a strange rumor spread. *The New York Times* had reported:

The May issue of French *Glamour* magazine contains a nude photo display of Isabella Rossellini, which was deemed too racy for the American market. The four pages with the most explicit photos, by Paolo Roversi, were cut out of the copies distributed in the United States and Britain.

"The reason it was taken out was the nudity," said a source involved with the magazine's distribution, who spoke on condition of anonymity. "The mood in this country right now is that you can't sell that stuff. Also, the June issue has a topless model on the cover that will be covered up with a sticker" in the United States.

Olivier Mayeras, the director of French *Glamour*, which is published by Condé Nast, said: "I put only 4,000 copies in the States. There are some countries where it's difficult to sell magazines with nudes. We don't want to sell nude pictures in the States for that reason, and also in Japan."

A spokesman for Ms. Rossellini, Allen Burry, said the actress and model was unaware of any problems with publishing the photographs in the United States. "She's seen a copy, and she likes it," he said.

Lancôme, the cosmetics company, has four pages of advertising featuring Ms. Rossellini in the same issue.

The rumor was that it had been Lancôme that had demanded the photos be censored. Here are the photos:

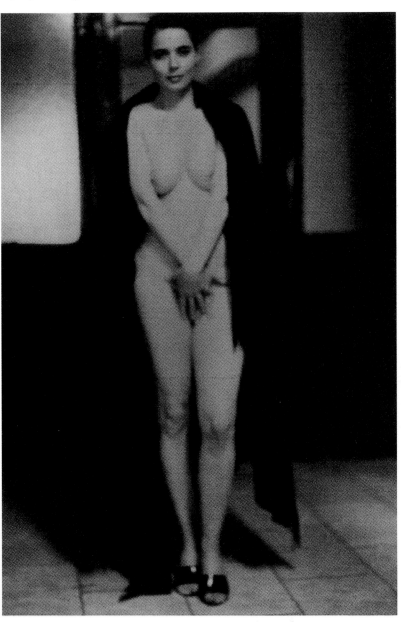

The "morals clause," the almost total exclusivity that compromised my choice of work, rang a bell. It reminded me of the old Hollywood contracts whereby the actors belonged to the studios and were not free players. It was the kind of contract my mother had had with David Selznick. I remember her telling me how much she had fought to make the films of her choice. After she had become a star, or as David Selznick saw it, after *he* had made her a star, he had leased her out to other film companies. My mom's salary was $60,000 a year, but Selznick was making sums such as $110,000 for *Casablanca*, $150,000 for *For Whom the Bell Tolls*, $100,000 for *Saratoga Trunk*.

"I didn't really mind. I'd signed a contract. I earned a lot more money than I ever had in Sweden. David didn't know I was going to be successful any more than I did. If he could make money renting me out, good luck to him," she wrote in her autobiography. But in 1946, she decided to become an independent artist and did not renew her agreement with Selznick. "I felt I had a right to some of the money he was making by renting me out." He got upset because he believed he had lifted her "from obscurity to great stardom," as he wrote to her in a memo. Mother became unhappy, because she looked up to him like a "father, my guide and leader." Selznick wrote to her, "This conclusion comes as no surprise to me, despite our final reliance and faith that I expressed in our conversation and in no way lessens my sorrow over our 'divorce' after so many years of happy marriage. You once said you had 'two husbands.' But Petter was the senior, and of course he knew all the time that his will would prevail. I do regret all the futile gestures and elaborate 'negotiations' but that is all I do regret in a relationship which will always be a source of pride to me."

Though I can't literally equate the forties' film agreements with today's exclusive top advertising contracts, there are similarities between the ways that actors then were working for the studio and I was working for the cosmetics company. Once I didn't serve the needs of the company any longer, I was to be dropped. If what defined me as a "model" had been only my work with Lancôme, once my Lancôme contract ended my career would have ended as well, just as an actor's career might have ended when the film studio decided it had.

I always knew I had to be as independent as I could in spite of the restrictions of the Lancôme contract. I insisted on doing as much editorial work as I could, and I wanted to act too. Film agents advised me against modeling and big advertising contracts: they're considered "not serious" for an actor. But in my case I believed modeling would work to my advantage. Because of my foreign accent in English, work in films and television had been precluded. I believe the glamour and familiarity of my face gained through modeling helped open up that opportunity for me in America. In fashion, where sight, not sound, counts, we all come from different countries, making it a much more international milieu than cinema—an aspect of fashion I've always appreciated and enjoyed, also because it reflects the way I grew up.

During all the years of my Lancôme contract, I constantly negotiated for more freedom, and my insistence on doing editorial photos had the added benefit of keeping me up to date on new photographers and talent that I could then suggest to Lancôme to work on new campaigns. To give you an idea of how many modifications, extensions, renewals, and renegotiations were done, to the left is a photo of how slim my first contract was and how thick it later became.

NEW WAYS

Models, when they break out of the continuing series of new, beautiful, anonymous girls discovered year after year by agencies, photographers, and designers, can have much longer careers. The supermodels of today have asserted themselves as personalities, and their names—Claudia Schiffer, Linda Evangelista, Kate Moss—have become as familiar as those of Hollywood stars. Mary Pickford had done that in the early years of film; until she arrived, actors were merely "players" and actresses were anonymous beauties. Though in modeling, the break from anonymity seems to be a revival of a trend: Veruschka, Twiggy, and Jean Shrimpton were household names in the sixties; models then went back to anonymity, only to find new success with the supermodel era.

The trend of supermodels influenced and modified my work with Lancôme during the fourteen years I worked for the company. At the beginning, I was just photographed—the new girl, the new Lancôme face, nobody wanted to know who I was or what my opinions were. But while our campaign was succeeding, models were acquiring status. They were the new stars. And my work in films was getting noticed. The department stores, always thinking of new ways to attract people, started asking Lancôme to have me make public appearances. The press demanded interviews, and requests to participate in and lend my name to different causes and benefits became a daily affair. Although my name was never printed in the ads, everybody knew it was me. . . .

I shouldn't say everybody knew it was me even if my name wasn't mentioned. In fact, at the time the termination of my contract was announced in the press, Lancôme had reserved the right to use all my photos for an "override" period of another year. My family and friends, unaware of the details of my deal, began telling me that the "new" girl didn't look at all as beautiful as I. The more perceptive wondered why Lancôme had chosen someone so similar to me but . . . "not as distinguished"!

In 1989, I signed a new contract with Lancôme for the perfume Trésor. The new agreement gave me many more responsibilities, including the right to get involved in all aspects of Trésor's creation, and I was to be paid a salary and a percentage of the sales—this, too, I borrowed from the movie business, where stars demand a percentage of a movie's earnings on top of their salary. Later, after my agreement with Lancôme ended, I adopted something else from the film industry: with Lancaster I signed a "development deal" just like the ones actors have with studios. Instead of committing to a particular film, or in my case to a cosmetics line, we are to develop the project together so that I have real input into it.

With my new Trésor agreement with Lancôme, my schedule changed radically. My days were no longer spent mostly in photography studios in New York, London, Paris, Miami, or L.A. Accompanied most of the time by the charming, efficient head of public relations at Lancôme, Claudine Clot-Desmet, I traveled to many places, including Spain, Germany, Belgium, Great Britain, Italy, France, Canada, Singapore, Japan, Taiwan, Mexico, Greece, Russia, the Scandinavian countries, and Hong Kong, as well as several U.S. cities, meeting the press and the sales forces by making numerous public appearances at various department stores.

In Taiwan, we were mobbed by a crowd, couldn't finish our

presentation, and had to leave with the help of the police through the underground corridors of the department store. In another Asian country, two hundred girls recruited from the countryside had been taught Western manners, nowadays considered the international standard. They were to be employed in airport duty-free shops and had to deal with clients of all nationalities. I was the "final exam." Each one had to greet me and shake my hand—not too softly, not too firmly, just right. They had to look me straight in the eye while speaking, a very difficult task if you've been brought up in a country where looking straight into people's eyes is considered an act of arrogant defiance. They were to keep their voices soft and in a low timbre and not slide up to the high pitch of local tradition.

I came to realize the power of what I symbolized—not only creams, beauty, and elegance but wealth, free economy, and work, so longed for in many countries. I was overwhelmed by the exhaustion of meeting five hundred to seven hundred people a day, but mostly by having so much emotion directed at me. These emotions ranged from just being in awe of me to defying me. The subtext of the usual "Hello, nice to meet you" had infinite shadings—they were all reacting to a personal idea they had formed about me. I had become an icon. Again I felt a familiarity with Mao. Not only were his famous sayings like a grandmother's recommendations—as I had learned on my long Chinese train trip—but his photos were everywhere, just like mine with Lancôme. The massive publicity campaign of Lancôme gave me a glimpse into the power these omnipresent images have. Dictators knew, before big capitalistic enterprise did, how to make use of it.

This is the most unreported aspect of a model/spokesperson's life, and it was the one that both touched me most and filled me with the most perplexity about our human nature and how we can be manipulated. Often at night, after one of these emotional days, I would cry in my bed, moved by the sea of people I had seen and by the hopes, fantasies, and feelings I knew my ever-present photos had inspired.

STYLE AND CONTENT

My dad was called "the father of neorealism." His work, I believe, paralleled in film the photography of Henri Cartier-Bresson, Chim Seymour, George Rodgers, and Robert Capa, the founders of the photographic agency Magnum. My mother admired—more, loved—Robert Capa. They had an affair I envied Mother for. When my mother first saw my father's films, I believe (I was not yet born, so this is just conjecture) she saw Robert Capa's photos come to life, moving. It was her opportunity to participate in something that she deeply respected and that was also totally different from Hollywood films. Her autobiography, written with Alan Burgess, starts, "She came out into the cold air of Hollywood's La Cienega Blvd. and she felt dazed. She looked at the glowing neon, the headlights of the passing traffic, and taking Petter's arm she urged him toward the Playbill outside the movie theatre saying, 'Petter, we must get this director's name straight. If there is such a man who can put this on the screen, he must be an absolutely heavenly human being.' "

When I asked my mother why she had begun her book like this, she replied, "Seeing *Open City* and the consequences of it was the most important event of my life."

She described the film: "The realism and simplicity of *Open City* were heart-shocking. No one looked like an actor, no one talked like an actor, there were darkness and shadows, and sometimes you couldn't hear and sometimes you couldn't even see it, but that's the way it is in life. . . . You can't always see and hear, but you know that something almost beyond understanding is going on. It was as if they had removed the walls from the houses and the rooms and you could see inside them. And it was more than that, it was as if you were there, involved in what was going on, and you wept and bled for them."

Because she was a prudent creature, Mother waited for my father's next film, *Paisan.* She was again very impressed, so she decided to write him and ask if they could work together.

They not only worked together in five films, but they fell in love and had three kids (including me). This created one of the biggest scandals of the century, and it marked my parents for life. They were banned from Hollywood—not officially, but when even the American Senate took a stand against them, declaring, "From the ashes of Ingrid Bergman a new Hollywood will be born," they decided to stay in Europe, where I grew up.

The first time I touched Hollywood soil, I was twenty-five years old. "Your father charged the price of a ticket to show what I can see free of charge right outside my door in the street," the concierge of the hotel in which I was staying told me as soon as I arrived. He still resented my father for "stealing," as he put it, my mother from Hollywood. His negative remarks finally helped me understand what it was about my father's films that irritated some people.

My father's features, in fact, seemed so authentic that often people thought they weren't feature films but a kind of documentary. Even the investors in *Open City* thought so and refused to pay him. "The contract calls for a film. This is reality. Why didn't you make a film?" And all the costs accumulated in the making of the film were debited to my father, who had to pay them through the years to come.

This would not be the last such time. Periodically while we were growing up, all our furniture would be confiscated by the authorities to pay his debts. They would leave the beds, but only the mattresses—the headboards went, too. I didn't think much about it. Only as an adult did I understand that this kind of thing was considered a "disgrace." I always perceived the problem as one that could be easily solved, and I love easy solutions. We bought all our furniture at the flea market (still one of my favorite ways of shopping), knowing that soon it would all be gone. Actually, I had had a glimpse of the concept of "disgrace" earlier on. I had seen my mother crying when the witch hat she had worn in Victor Fleming's *Joan of Arc,* in the scene where she is marched to the stake amid a screaming crowd, was confiscated. She had made it into a lampshade, so it fell into the "disgraced" category of furniture and was snatched away by the authorities to pay debts.

At any rate, my father's films revolutionized cinema. (I'm pretty sure about that—I don't think a daughter's love makes me perceive his importance as greater than it actually was.) Dad couldn't stand critics and film scholars. He hated their endless debates, reasoning, and arguing about film styles, and most of all he was exasperated about his so-called new style, labeled "neorealism." He despised the importance given to form over content: "I never decide first what style I'm going to make my film in. First I decide what I want to say, then I see how. It's the content and how much money the producer gives me that determines the style of my film, not the other way around."

This is how I grew up—despising the word "style"—and that's the principal reason why I resisted becoming a model until I was twenty-eight, by which time many women have stopped modeling. I believed that fashion and cosmetics had to do only with style, never with content. But eventually I came to question this. There is some unknown force that makes us move all together in one direction or another, toward a given style. It's a fascinating mystery, and slowly I came to question my dad's opinion. Style? Why not? It's a pleasant phenomenon. Even if it's only style and no content.

A CAN OF WORMS

None of the artists I've ever met—no photographer, director, fashion designer—has ever talked about why they did things the way they did. They make vague remarks. If it's an artist from the fashion world, chances are a "Gorgeous" or a "Divine" will pop out; if it's David Lynch, it will be a "Geez, Louise" or a "Holy jumping George"; if it's someone as introverted as photographer Paolo Roversi, nothing will be said at all, just profound silence. It is the critics, the journalists, the people on the other side of the creative force who try to explain, analyze, give definition, declare that a new style has come into vogue, pushing another one out of vogue. By baptizing a tendency, they create a kind of corral around it: neorealism, expressionism, nineties women, and so on. Artists themselves, I think, don't like definitions because they're a way of imposing rules and regulations that inevitably confine them and make them feel trapped.

"Do you think that *After Hours* is a real Scorsese film?" I was once asked. It reminded me of a discussion involving Freud and other luminaries: "In your last writing your theory doesn't seem Freudian . . ." The answer came: "But I *am* Freud."

I couldn't refrain from making the same mistake, and instead of just letting things be I did a lot of reasoning and rationalizing, used a lot of words and theories, especially when it came to Rossellini, Scorsese, and Lynch. I refer to them as my personal Trinity. I wanted them to like one another and I didn't want them to argue, so I tried very hard to corral them into definitions and find a common denominator that would reconcile their differences. Though in reality they never fought. My dad never met Martin or David: he died before I'd fallen in love with one and then the other a few years later. David and Martin don't know each other. But in my imaginary conversations I feared that their differences could lead to quarrels, and I did not want this to happen to the family in my heart.

My father leads these imaginary discussions by giving me long, long lectures—quite like sermons, I would say. He did that when he was alive, too. He repeated his beliefs endlessly, drilling them into us. His teachings were so strong that sometimes my brothers, sisters, and I were made to feel as if we belonged to a small cult with Father as the prophet and us as the followers. It never discouraged us to think we were just a handful of people. Even Jesus started with only twelve disciples.

THE SERMONS

"Listen, Sgionfa Bosse"—that's the nickname my dad had for me in the Venetian dialect of his mother. It means "the glass-blower." As a child I had cheeks as round and puffed out as those of any glass artisan of Murano. "See, Sgionfa Bosse, anatomically the cerebellum is the oldest and strongest part of the brain. The cortical area is the newest part, the most delicate as well as the most advanced. That's where thoughts, memory, imagination lie. Men always feel the weight of responsibility for this part of the brain and often try to put it to sleep, even using extreme methods such as alcohol and drugs. This tendency always existed, but it's more violent in the modern world because our responsibilities are greater . . ." And on he would go with his scientific explanation.

My dad loved science. He intended to make films about biology, chemistry, physics—not documentaries but feature films. I contributed to his research for a scientific feature film by plunging into the Mediterranean to fish for urchins—male and female—in order to open them up, take out their eggs and sperm, mix them in a dish, and put them under a microscope, which was placed in our kitchen so that he could film the fertilization.

What I saw was many small, frantic sperm attacking a big, immobile, round egg. As soon as one sperm penetrated the egg, it disappeared as if it had dissolved into it. The only indication that its entrance had had an effect was that immediately a ring appeared around the egg like a tougher layer. And then *"blub,"* as I mimicked the sound I associated with what I was seeing to Father, the mixture (egg plus sperm) inside the ring divided into two, and then *blub, blub,* each of the two parts divided again. And then the four parts divided into eight. At this point everything usually stopped. You know, each part would have kept on dividing and specializing, becoming the urchin's spikes, the beak, the flesh we eat, or, if it was an egg and sperm from humans, the leg, the head, the heart. But in contact with the kitchen air, everything quickly died. My dad never completed his feature film about science. He had been thinking about it and experimenting to figure out how to make it when he himself died.

One of Father's most repeated sermons was about Comenius, who, in 1670, complained about the limitations of language: "If you had to describe an elephant to people who had never seen one, you would have to use an immense number of words and still, since words are not precise, 'large,' 'gray,' 'long nose' will conjure up different ideas of how big is big, what shade of gray, how long is a long nose, et cetera. The result being that we all have a different idea of what an elephant is, which probably has nothing to do with the reality. But if you show an elephant, you can understand precisely and instantly what it looks like. Film can do that—it's the greatest instrument for information. With film, ignorance in the world can be defeated," my father would say, lighting up with enthusiasm. "The technological discoveries of this century are as big as the discovery of fire for the primitive world. Many people believe that man is motivated by two impulses: fear and desire. I would add knowledge. This is my definition of man: it's an erect creature who wants to stand on his toes to look further out to the horizon."

My mind often gives me flashes of Papa attacking modern artists:

"Do they still believe they can find the truth—all the big answers to life—attached to the lower belly between their legs?"

Or he might thunder:

"All these *auteurs de cinéma*, these directors of independent films, art movies, whatever filmmakers are called nowadays, who want to free themselves from the power of money and the conventions of commercial films—are they still spilling their guts all over the place so that we can watch in fascination or at best identify with them?"

Or:

"Is it still the dark side—what Marx called the 'nonhuman' and Freud the 'id,' the part of us which if we unleash it will make us just fuck, eat, drink, and kill—that provides the artistic inspiration for your beloved ones?"

I never quite understand what he means when he calls on people like Marx and Freud. I never read as much as he did, but it's his "your beloved ones" that freezes the blood in my veins, because, you see, it's the dark side, the inexplicable, the mystery that has been David's inspiration.

To make things worse, David proudly called himself an "artist," a word my dad hated. David kept telling me he wanted to live "the life of the arts," and my dad used to say, "I don't want to be called an artist, I don't even want to be one. I try to be a man. I can't stand these artists who think their original point of view about the world is what counts. They try to make everything different, original. They call themselves talented as if they were kissed by God, wrapped in inspiration. . . . All the problems of the world come from this trying to be different, trying to stand out—it leads to sensationalism—instead of going to the world with the courage and the humility to be a man."

One day I read a definition of German Expressionism. It said something like "Expressionism is the search for the truth, the truth in the soul, not the truth in front of your eyes. The faces in the paintings are slightly exaggerated, like a caricature, to capture in the features what lies deep in the soul." I showed it to David. "Is that what you're doing?" I asked, happy to have found a definition that I hoped could redeem him and absolve him from my father's inquisition. David seemed to think this was a definition that could somehow be applied to his work, but he didn't pay much attention; probably he wasn't interested in being categorized.

From the glazed expression he often had in his eyes, I could always deduce when he wasn't listening to me. I suspect he lingers in other dimensions. One of his nicknames, in fact, is "the Jimmy Stewart from Mars."

When we did *Blue Velvet,* David had a phrase for me to help me conjure up Dorothy Vallens's mood swings, tormented mind, and anguish: "The clouds are coming." When we created Dorothy, I already knew about battered women, and I gathered more information before playing the role. I inquired into sadomasochism, and I went deep inside me, into the confusion, fear, and helplessness I had felt in eliciting sexual desire and attraction when I had been a beautiful young girl. I summoned up my memory of the trauma of date rape I had experienced and even a mysterious firmament that had appeared to me once when I had been brutally beaten. I had felt no pain, just total surprise. I remember the first blow, and then I saw darkness with little lights, a bit like Donald Duck when he gets hit over the head. When I played Dorothy, asking to be beaten, I recalled those stars. The way of stopping the anguished thoughts—"the clouds"—was to be hit and be bewildered in front of this firmament. This is how I understood Dorothy's sadomasochism and how I joined the surrealism and poetry of David Lynch's world.

I can describe working with David as: one, two, three—leap into the void. One, two, three is what's earthbound, and it has to be totally real and plausible. Like a good runway, it allows a leap into a mysterious world that may hold deeper truths. It's not a love of the strange and unusual that dictates David's surrealistic style; it's as if our rational minds can go only so far, and then intuition is needed in order to float further into the mysterious, transcendental, inexplicable.

A GOOD DIRECTOR

This is a slightly indiscreet story, but it's the clearest example I have to describe what constitutes a good director. When David left me, I was totally brokenhearted. I surprised even myself at how depressed I became. I didn't seem able to climb out of my black pit. But there is always some light in every situation, so I decided to look for it. Whatever I find that is positive, however thin and faint, I will hang on to it and, like threads in fairy tales, use it to come out of the woods. But the only positive thing that came to mind was that possibly Martin would be pleased to know about it. Not that Martin was nostalgic about me, not at all, but you know . . . just that strange sense of possession that lingers even after divorce . . .

I found Martin in Venice, at the annual film festival there.

MARTIN SCORSESE AND ME

"Martin, David left me," I said on the phone. "I knew it," he announced, to my complete surprise. "How did you know? None of us knew—none of my friends, none of my family expected it, and it was the furthest thing from my mind. How did you know?" "I knew it when I saw you and David on the news, at the Cannes Film Festival. When David won the Palme d'Or for *Wild at Heart*, he kissed you on the lips in front of the press." "So what?" "Well, you've both been so very discreet about your relationship, even if everybody knew you were together—there haven't been any photos, any declarations. If David chose to display his love to you in front of the press after the five years you were together, he obviously had something to hide."

See what I mean? Good directors know about human behavior. When I hung up the phone, I didn't feel at all consoled. I didn't feel I'd found the end of the thread I could start to follow to come out of the woods of my depression, but along with my sadness at having lost David, I had an astounding admiration for the perspicacity and acuteness that is required of good directors. I had thought that David had finally relaxed and had believed after so many years that we could finally, officially be a couple. My lack of insight on that occasion makes me wonder if I can indeed direct one day, because, see, I've thought of doing that too.

DAVID LYNCH AND ME

THE INSPIRATION

When David was asked in a press conference where he had gotten the idea for *Blue Velvet,* he answered disarmingly, "In my chair." His candor and matter-of-fact simplicity enchanted me. Later, he elaborated a little for me; explanation, though, is not his forte. "I sit and wait for an idea to come. It's a bit like fishing . . ." Slowly, following his awkward explanation, images appeared in my brain, and this is the way I imagine David's creative process to be. Sitting there, doing nothing, staring at a wall of his sparsely furnished house, his mind starts up. Disconnected thoughts, images, colors appear, and then one of them strikes and surprises the semistunned David. A "fish" is caught. "You need not leave your room. Remain sitting at your table and listen. You need not even listen. Simply wait. You need not even wait. Just learn to become quiet and still and solitary. The world will freely offer itself to you to be unmasked." What Kafka wrote, I suspect, is what David calls "fishing." To lead the caught fish to him, David has to gently pull and release, pull and release, and so he does with his idea, indulging it and slowly forming a story.

For Martin, I think, the process is different. There is always a book, an already written script, a biography that interests him. But to become his, that story has to go through the sieve of his soul, not an easy process. I imagine this story taking a trip like Dante's through Inferno, Purgatory, and Paradise.

As for Daddy, he denied having any intimate psychological or personal involvement with his films.

FATHER: I TRY TO BE OBJECTIVE. FILM WHAT I SEE.

MARTIN: OBJECTIVE FILMMAKING, SUBJECTIVE FILMMAKING, ALL THAT ARGU-
MENT IS SO CONFUSING . . .

FATHER: WELL, JUST LET ME SAY THEN THAT, FOR EXAMPLE, I DO NOT BE-LONG TO THAT CATEGORY OF FILMMAKERS WHOSE ULTIMATE GOAL IS TO TALK ABOUT THEMSELVES, USING SOMEONE ELSE'S LIFE OR STORY AS A PRE-TEXT FOR DOING SO.

ISABELLA: WHAT ARE YOU TALKING ABOUT?

I hate it whenever there is even the slightest polemic tone in the voices in my head.

FATHER: WHEN I DID MY FILM *THE MESSIAH*, I WAS CRITICIZED: "WHAT WOULD HAVE MADE IT AN INTERESTING FILM WOULD HAVE BEEN IF YOU, ROSSELLINI, HAD TOLD US WHAT YOU THOUGHT AND FELT ABOUT THE MES-SIAH." BUT WHAT WOULD THAT MATTER? WHY ARE MY PERSONAL OPINIONS AND THOUGHTS INTERESTING? I WANTED TO RELATE WHAT CHRIST SAID— ISN'T THAT MORE IMPORTANT? AND YET I WAS ACCUSED OF MAKING A COLD FILM, AND THIS COLDNESS WAS VIEWED SOMEHOW AS ANTIRELIGIOUS AND THE FILM DID NOT GET DISTRIBUTED.

ISABELLA: PAPA, DO YOU THINK THAT MARTIN IN *THE LAST TEMPTATION OF CHRIST* WAS JUST USING CHRIST TO EXPRESS HIS OWN DOUBTS AND FEEL-INGS ABOUT RELIGION AND GOD AND MAN?

FATHER: IT'S A POSSIBILITY.

ISABELLA: MARTIN, DID YOU DO THAT?

And Martin's imaginary voice answers:

MARTIN: IDENTIFYING WITH JESUS—THE MAN, NOT THE GOD—AND FINDING A COMMON DENOMINATOR AMONG ALL US HUMANS—ISN'T THAT THE ONLY WAY WE'VE GOT TO UNDERSTAND ONE ANOTHER? I HAVE ONLY ONE WAY TO CONVEY HUMAN DOUBT, TROUBLE, OPPOSITE PULLS, AND THAT IS BY USING MYSELF AS A DEPARTURE POINT.

FATHER: ISN'T THIS THE LIMITATION OF MODERN ARTISTS?

Wait, I've got to explain this. My father, now that he's dead, sees things from the scale of time that belongs to that world: eternity. For him, a hundred years is nothing. From his perspective, it just takes me and him, a father and a daughter, to cover an entire century. He was born in 1906, when there were no cars, no telephones, no electricity in the houses. When cars arrived, his mother had no foresight at all: "It's a fad, they won't last, they smell too bad." And when my father died, there were no VCRs, no video stores, no CNN to show news all over the world, even in countries with heavy censorship, no home computers, no supersonic planes for ordinary passengers, all things I use normally (supersonic planes, though, only in the richest moments of my life). If I live until 2006, which is likely—I'd be only fifty-four years old then—together we will have covered the entire hundred years of the century. So for my father, an argument that's maybe one or two hundred years old is still worth discussing.

ISABELLA: MARTIN, "ISN'T THIS THE LIMITATION OF MODERN ARTISTS?" REFERS TO THAT ARGUMENT THAT STARTED WITH ROMANTICISM, WHEN ARTISTS WERE FIRST SEEN AS CENTRAL FIGURES, INDIVIDUALS WITH SPECIAL SENSITIVITY AND AN ABILITY TO EXPRESS THE MOODS OF THEIR GENERATION THROUGH THEIR ART. MYSTERIOUS EVENTS, WHICH ONLY THEY EXPERIENCED, LIKE INSPIRATION—

FATHER (INTERRUPTING ME): INSPIRATION! I NEVER GOT ANY. DO YOU, MARTIN?

Inspiration? David would know the answer—he would talk about "fishing"—but in my imaginary conversations I never have David talk to my parents. Not after I took my clothes off in *Blue Velvet*.

FATHER: WHAT IS THIS "INSPIRATION"? I JUST FEEL LIKE A SIMPLE CHAP WHO PUTS ONE FOOT IN FRONT OF THE OTHER AND STEP BY STEP ATTEMPTS TO UNDERSTAND AND KNOW MORE. ONCE I GET HOLD OF A FEW CONCEPTS I MAKE A FILM ABOUT THEM TO SHARE MY UNDERSTANDING WITH OTHERS. THIS IS THE ESSENCE OF ALL MY FILMS.

Now even my mother's voice joins in:

MOTHER: ROBERTO, IT'S THE WAY YOU SHARE YOUR KNOWLEDGE, YOUR STORIES, YOUR EMOTIONS THAT COUNTS. A STORY CAN BE ENJOYED ONLY IF IT'S TOLD WELL. THE SAME STORY TOLD BY SOMEONE ELSE COULD BE TOTALLY UNINTERESTING. IN ART, ONLY FORM COUNTS.

FATHER: A FILM WELL MADE, A STORY WELL TOLD, THAT'S THE MINIMUM TO EXPECT—IT'S JUST BEING PROFESSIONAL. WHAT COUNTS IS WHAT YOU SAY. ON THE OTHER HAND, IT'S IMPORTANT TO LEARN TO BE A GOOD LISTENER. ONE SHOULDN'T KNEEL TO THE COMMERCIAL DEMANDS OF STANDARDIZATION OF HOW TO TELL A STORY. OTHERWISE WE RISK DISMISSING, FOR EXAMPLE, A BRILLIANT STUTTERER WITH GREAT THINGS TO SAY BECAUSE HIS DELIVERY IS IMPAIRED.

MARTIN: ROSSELLINI . . .

(That's how Martin would refer to my dad, because he knows him more as a filmmaker than as his father-in-law.)

MARTIN (CONTINUED): . . . YOUR CHOICE OF FILMING SO SIMPLY, SO IMPASSIVELY, DOES IT COME FROM YOUR FAITH THAT PEOPLE WILL LISTEN AS LONG AS SOMETHING INTERESTING IS BEING TOLD?

FATHER: I HAVE TOTAL FAITH IN THAT. IF I HAVE SOMETHING INTERESTING TO SAY, THE MOST EFFICIENT WAY TO SAY IT IS THE SIMPLEST, MOST DIRECT WAY. I DON'T NEED TO SURPRISE OR OVERWHELM MY AUDIENCE WITH FANCY EFFECTS TO GRAB THEIR ATTENTION, TO MANIPULATE THEIR EMOTIONS. THAT KIND OF FLASHY FILMMAKING IS OFTEN USED TO COVER UP FAULTS IN THE CONTENT.

MARTIN: I LIKE IT FLASHY. I LIKE TO GRAB MY AUDIENCE AND FORCE THEM TO WATCH. WHY NOT USE IT ALL? SOLID STORIES, TOLD IN THE FLASHIEST, MOST GRIPPING WAY . . .

When I was married to Martin Scorsese and went to visit him on the set for the first time, I was taken aback by his complicated camera moves and his numerous setups to cover a scene. The way you choose to express yourself in words, in films, even where and how you live, what clothes you wear, defines who you are—it's a revelation of your morality. I grew up believing that the morally correct placing of the camera in films was at eye level and because it was morally correct it was elegant. Elegance, even when applied to a well-dressed woman, conveys to me an idea of correctness and moral righteousness.

My brother Renzo once placed the camera just a bit higher than eye level to give a sense of royal splendor when filming the extravagant meals in Father's film *The Rise of Louis XIV*. My dad, unlike all the other directors I've known, often fled the set, which I think bored him, leaving my elder brother with rigid instructions on how to direct the scenes. Renzo was trembling when those scenes were screened the following day, but luckily my father never noticed his disobedience. If he had, he would have thundered, "What kind of filmmaking is that? Like a TV commercial subliminally influencing your audience in order to manipulate their emotions and grab their attention in a sneaky way instead of honestly showing events just as your eyes would have perceived them if you had lived in 1700."

When I observed Martin's celebrated camera moves—the ones, for example, plunging into the actors from a direct angle above them—I thought, "It's a point of view only a fly could have," and I was filled with perplexity and debates in my head about whether it was "morally" correct. When I saw Martin's films completed, I felt he didn't use the camera simply like an eye but more like music. The camera moves were choreographed to be emotional comments on the scenes. To further my puzzlement, Martin's and Father's films, which are executed so differently, feel similar to me. They are real, "as if they had removed the walls from the houses and the rooms and you could see inside them," to quote how my mother in her autobiography described my dad's work.

MARTIN: WHEN I WAS A KID AND WENT TO THE MOVIES, I DIDN'T EXPECT FILMS TO RELATE TO WHAT WAS AROUND ME. I LOVED THE EXPERIENCE OF BEING MESMERIZED, HYPNOTIZED BY THEM.

FATHER: JEAN RENOIR WAS ONE OF MY CLOSEST FRIENDS. TALKING ABOUT THE POWER OF FILM LANGUAGE, HE WOULD TELL ME, "WHAT MATTERED TO ME WAS A FINE CLOSE-UP. IT SO HAPPENED THAT THE PUBLIC, TO ACCEPT A CLOSE-UP, HAD TO BE GIVEN A STORY. . . . I BOWED TO THE NECESSITY . . . BUT WITH RELUCTANCE." I THOUGHT THAT WAS VERY AMUSING. I WOULD ASK, "JEAN, WERE YOU READY TO BEAR WITH THE MOST TEDIOUS FILM JUST TO SEE A CLOSE-UP OF AN ACTRESS YOU LIKED?" "YES." AND WE WOULD BOTH ROAR WITH LAUGHTER AT THE MEMORY OF WHAT WE NOW CONSIDER A YOUTHFUL WAY OF LOVING FILMS. THOUGH I UNDERSTAND THE POWER OF CLOSE-UPS. IN "THE HUMAN VOICE" I KEPT THE CAMERA ON ANNA MAGNANI'S FACE ALL THE TIME. I WANTED THE CAMERA TO BE LIKE A MICROSCOPE AND SEE ALL THE WAY INSIDE HER.

MARTIN: IT WAS THIS POWER OF FILM LANGUAGE THAT MADE ME WANT TO BECOME A FILMMAKER. AT FIRST I WAS ONLY FAMILIAR WITH AMERICAN FILMS, THEN, LATER ON, I WENT TO FILM SCHOOL AND I SAW THE EUROPEAN FILMS. THEY HIT ME WITH THE POWER OF A SLEDGEHAMMER, THEY WERE SO MUCH FREER IN CONTENT AND FORM. NOT HAVING A STUDIO SYSTEM, THE WAY WE DID IN AMERICA, THEY COULD MAKE FILMS THAT WERE MORE INDIVIDUALISTIC. DIRECTORS WERE RECOGNIZED AS AUTHORS. I TRY TO PUT INTO MY WORK EVERYTHING I LOVE IN FILMS AND MORE. I USE ALL I HAVE AND ALL AT MAXIMUM POWER, LOUD AND BOLD LIKE ROCK AND ROLL.

FATHER: I GET DISTURBED BY TOO MUCH FLASH. I RESENT BEING MANIPULATED. WHAT FILLS ME WITH GREAT EMOTION IN LIFE IS THAT THE MOST DRAMATIC MOMENTS HAPPEN IN THE SAME MANNER AS NORMAL, EVERYDAY EVENTS. IT'S THIS HUMBLE, SPARE, CHILLING QUALITY THAT I TRY TO TRANSCRIBE IN MY FILMS.

MARTIN: THE WAY YOU DID IN *VIAGGIO IN ITALIA*. I LOVE THAT FILM.

MOTHER: IN *VIAGGIO IN ITALIA* I JUST HAD TO WALK AROUND LOOKING AT ITALY'S BEAUTIFUL MONUMENTS, NATURE, AND PEOPLE. I WAS SO BORED! GODARD AND TRUFFAUT TOLD ME HOW MUCH THIS FILM INFLUENCED THEIR *NOUVELLE VAGUE*. I NEVER QUITE UNDERSTOOD THAT. AND YOU LIKE IT TOO, MARTIN? MANY PEOPLE IN HOLLYWOOD BELIEVED THAT ROBERTO RUINED MY CAREER WITH FILMS LIKE THAT. I FELT I RUINED HIS. I FEARED I WAS FORCING HIM TO WRITE FILMS FOR ME BECAUSE, DUE TO THE GREAT SCANDAL WE HAD CREATED BY FALLING IN LOVE, I COULDN'T WORK IN AMERICA ANY LONGER. *EUROPA 51, STROMBOLI, VIAGGIO IN ITALIA* WERE NOT SUCCESSFUL AND, MOST IMPORTANT, I DIDN'T FEEL ANYTHING SPECIAL FOR THEM. THEY DIDN'T MOVE ME AS *OPEN CITY* OR *PAISAN*, THE VERY FILMS THAT MADE ME LEAVE HOLLYWOOD TO JOIN HIM.

FATHER: YOU NEVER UNDERSTOOD THE FILMS WE DID TOGETHER . . .

. . . and here lies the big conflict between my parents, which I believe led to their divorce. I don't know all the reasons my parents broke up, but I suspect artistic differences played a part. Mother always admired and respected Father's work. My father didn't always respect Mother's choices, though he always admired her talent as an actress. Mother believed in the force of talent; Father believed that talent *tout court* didn't deserve being as celebrated as it is. She believed in entertainment in the classic Hollywood sense; Father was bored by it.

MARTIN: IN FACT, ROSSELLINI, YOU STAND ASIDE. YOU DON'T REALLY BELONG TO WHAT IS GENERALLY REFERRED TO AS THE WORLD OF FILMMAKERS OR ENTERTAINMENT.

FATHER: I ALWAYS SUSPECTED THAT. I HAD A FOLLOWING OF PEOPLE WHO LOVED, EVEN WORSHIPED, MY WORK, BUT I DIDN'T TRUST THESE "ROSSELLINIANS." I SUSPECTED THAT THEIR LOVE WAS BASED MOSTLY ON AESTHETIC GROUNDS, AND I COULDN'T CARE LESS ABOUT THOSE. MY FILMS ARE TOTALLY BASED ON MORAL CHOICES. I GUESS YOU'RE RIGHT, MARTIN, I'M NOT REALLY A FILMMAKER THAT WAY. I'M RELIEVED TO ADMIT IT. MY JOB IS TO BE A MAN; THAT'S ALL.

HUMOR

I wish my mind could also give me the way my father spoke, because it was light, brilliant, imaginative, and full of humor.

He would conjure up the most creative sentences, insults, and comparisons. Here are a few examples I've collected from interviews he gave:

- Describing film director Marcel Pagnol: "He was the most joyous and good-humored person. He fireworked words and stories, one funnier than the next."
- About grammar: "All these rules we have to learn in school that are called names that buzz like flies."
- Commenting on director Vittorio De Sica's majestic funeral: "This is the last time I will come to a funeral as an amateur."
- About a dinner: "There were more intellectuals at dinner than pigeons in Piazza San Marco."
- To a stylish gay director who irritated him beyond belief: "I will sew up your asshole."
- In Paris after the war, describing Jean Cocteau, Paul Claudel, Pagnol, Renoir: "They sparkled intelligence like a wooden fire."
- About the mythic French actress Mistinguett, he told journalist Stefano Roncoroni for their book, *Quasi un'autobiografia*: "She must have been eighty-two years old. She was the embodiment of fragility. Her cheeks looked like cocker spaniel's ears, and her legs were so shaky that in order to stand she had to be held up by a chorus of young boys who would kick her in the ass to make her swing one way or the other to make it look as if she was still capable of dancing. The audience emanated immense love for her and showered her with applause. At the end of the show Mistinguett ap-

peared, holding herself up at the curtain in order to stand. She was incredibly stingy and took advantage of the chat with the audience to do the shopping for the next day by asking, 'Is there a butcher among you? I'd love a ground steak. Would it be possible to get a little bit of it? Is there a baker among you . . . ?' The public, electrified by love and admiration, brought her so many presents she was forced to sell a few the next day."

REALITY VERSUS IMAGINATION

Father let his delightful fantasy and imagination roar and run at full speed like his Ferrari only in his personal life. For his work he restrained it, using it as only one of the tools of his filmmaking. "The stories I told, for example, in my so-called neorealistic films are not totally real, not totally invented—they are probable," he would state in interviews. He needed his imagination to invent and create that probability. He needed his imagination for his historical films to re-create their everyday atmosphere. But his films were based on reality and meticulously correct historically.

"You have to have a devilish amount of vanity to think that your own imagination is more astounding than reality. Our imagination doesn't go far. Reality is vast, more incredible, more varied than anything that comes out of our brain," Jean Renoir quotes his father, the great Impressionist painter Auguste, as saying in the biography he wrote of him.

This quote could be my father's, too. He believed that if you look carefully and deeply into anything, you'll see marvels. For him, nothing was uninteresting. To quote Jean further, giving an example to illustrate his father's insight: ". . . in the eye of a true horseman a horse is never black or white. . . . The hair of [its] coat is mixed. It's the combination of tones seen as a whole that gives the impression of the horse coat being black. . . . Among the countless hairs in it, even black comes in different pigments." Impressionists did not paint "impressions," as the name given by critics may suggest, but revealed deeper, previously unnoticed realities. Close observation allowed them to see the endless varieties and combinations of nature.

On the one hand, the marvel of reality enchanted my dad and humbled him (this reaction he used for his films); on the other, it inflamed his imagination (and this reaction he mostly reserved for us). Father's enthusiasm at finding a reddish hair in an apparently black horse coat could have led him to see and describe the animal to us as vermilion. For the last documentary he did, he climbed up the dome of Saint Peter's Cathedral and told us he had seen all the birds who had been in captivity and escaped from their cages living peacefully up there. "An unbelievable phenomenon!" he said. "There were parrots, canaries, finches, crows. It looked like a jungle." My dad also saw whales just outside our beach house in Santa Marinella, although no whales live in the Mediterranean. He would even hear their heavy breathing at night and get upset at us for not being able to see and hear what he did.

ABOUT LIES AGAIN

My dad's imagination, restrained only in his work, was otherwise boundless and often overwhelmed reality. If I were to say he lied, he would strike me with lightning, so please let me not use that word to describe what he did. Whatever Dad did . . . let's not give it a name . . . don't think he did it because he was an artist. Martin's films and, even more so, David's are full of fantasy, but in life they did not . . . you know what I want to say . . . do it to the extent of my daddy.

My mother, unlike my father, stuck to the truth—exaggeratedly so, I would say. You couldn't even ask her to tell a so-called polite lie, such as "Isabella's not here right now. Can she call you back?" for an unwanted phone call. She would not do it. If Mother answered the phone, you knew you had to take the call or she would say "Isabella does not want to talk to you." Her honesty was embarrassing. At home, we were all aware of this danger and had to behave accordingly.

I do not follow her example. I use my imagination, coloratura, lies, however you want to classify what I do, freely, like my dad, but then immediately feel an urge to admit to it with a very Bergman-like honesty. That's maybe being their daughter—the genetic result of a blend of Father and Mother.

HELPFUL LIES

My father used to say "my mother-in-love" or "my brother-in-love," referring to his mother-in-law and brother-in-law. Before he could be corrected, he was off praising the English language for this warm and sentimental definition of acquired family members. Because no one dared contradict him—he was very authoritarian—and no one had the heart to disappoint him that his sentimental "in-love" was instead the bureaucratical "in-law," the entire family adopted his mistaken way.

But for me, Flo, Elettra's grandmother, truly deserves the definition "mother-in-love." When I became pregnant with Elettra, I was married not to Jonathan but to Martin. That shocked many people, though not the three of us. Even so, we decided to give things the appearance of order. I divorced Martin and married Jonathan all in the same half hour in Santo Domingo, where an instant divorce, which costs $500, and an instant marriage, which costs $50 (very revealing of what people want most), can be obtained. That was a great relief, most of all to Lancôme and to Jonathan's family. As for me, I was slightly irritated at having to give in to what I considered absurd rules, bureaucracy, useless paperwork, and red tape. Martin was hurt, not because I'd had an affair—we'd split up long before—but because I'd broken my promise based on our friendship that we would stay married forever to protect him from further marriages. I was already his third. Jonathan was hurt because I didn't at all understand his value system, which respected the marital institution, and he wanted a more romantic bride than I. He gave me the most beautiful wedding ring, designed by my friend Susan Reinstein, and said, "You don't have to wear it." But I did.

When things went back to this more acceptable pattern—marriage, divorce, new marriage, baby—I was flooded with presents. They all came from Jonathan's family and friends in Texas: crystal glasses and vases, cookbooks, a Cuisinart, silver trays, monogrammed silverware, and so on. Overwhelmed, I stopped opening

JONATHAN'S BEAR, DOUGLAS, WITH MY DOLL, CATAVERINO, WEARING MY WEDDING RING

packages that came to the house, and boxes began piling up against a wall, eventually reaching the ceiling. Flo, Jonathan's mother, was called in to help, and I realized she had provoked the flock of presents: she had announced our marriage formally in Dallas. For her most conservative friends, who were ready to blame her and her child rearing for Jonathan's dissolute marriage to a married broad older than he was, she had made up a scenario: we had had a very, very private and romantic wedding in the south of France all alone in order to avoid the devouring and insatiable demands of the press. To confirm this scenario, she had cut out a Bruce Weber photo from a magazine that was part of a Lancôme campaign in which I was wearing a white hat, and she put it in a silver frame, pretending it was a photo of me in my wedding dress.

Flo arrived in New York armed with official cards to be sent back with "thank-you words" to her friends. On this stationery she had intertwined the initials "I" and "R" plus the added "W" for Wiedemann, all in an unintelligible scribble. The inscrutability was intended to avoid my fury—she knew I had no intention of changing my last name to Jonathan's—as well as to keep her friends from lifting their eyebrows again or too high about this refusal of mine. Her Machiavellian lies enchanted me. It was my first real contact with Jonathan's family. Through lies she won my confidence.

Flo helped me understand that she was not a victim of social rules, nor did she want me to become one. She respected the rules in order to show her respect for others. Just as a good, fun dance is one you know the steps to, rules allow a good, fun social life. Assured that my own freedom was going to be respected, I opened up to a mentality that was unknown to me—actually, a mentality I had resisted. I had defended myself

My PRETEND WEDDING
PHOTO

against the rituals of engagements, marriages, eternal love, maternal sacrifices, but thanks to Flo, I can now not only go to funerals—the only tradition I never questioned—but enjoy other official gatherings—marriages, shower parties, engagement parties—and share the excitement of a friend who is about to get married.

Don't think it was the frequent divorces, the homosexuality, the extramarital affairs with the creation of half brothers and sisters around the world all taking place within my family that forced me into being disrespectful of tradition and adopting unconventional attitudes. My pets helped a great deal. Once you've lived with dogs, cats, rabbits, birds, pigs, you've seen it all.

Gaitto, the male cat, has been raped by anything that has come into our house—dogs, rabbits, ferrets, pigs. Only the goldfish, confined in its bowl, spared him—and Pongo, my nephew Tommaso's parrot, who we believed was male until he started to lay eggs. Macaroni, my daughter's dog, is the mother of eight Jack Russell puppies. (Actually, we call them "Jack Rossellinis" because they're slightly different from Jack Russells; they have short legs and

are complete—with long tails and dewclaws, because we didn't cut them.) When it comes to sex, Macaroni takes on the male role, though, and goes for Gaitto and now for the young male cat, Tatto.

Pets make you face the darkest, most hidden facts of nature. There have been sex crossings, species crossings, even sex with inanimate objects—my furniture—at home. Spanky, my pig, humped the living room furniture every night. In the morning, everything had to be put back where it belonged: the sofa in front of the fireplace, the chairs around the dining table, the pillows back on the sofas, and so on.

When I was a kid, I picked up every stray I found in the streets and kept it in my bedroom. Once when I entered my room I saw something that resembled Alka-Seltzer in water—the bed, the curtains, the rug, everything was fizzing. It was a cheerful sight until I realized that the fizz was the fleas from the four dogs I'd collected. My dad told me I would be sent to boarding school if I kept bringing dogs in from the street. I kept bringing them. He did not send me to boarding school.

When I turned twenty-one, mother offered to buy me a fur coat. She wanted to keep some sort of traditional order in our very disordered family:

- The watch for my First Communion. Got it.
- The little pearl necklace at sixteen. Got it and lost it.
- The debutante party at eighteen. I refused, too embarrassing.
- The fur coat at twenty-one. No, thanks . . .

So she had to think what else she could give me to mark this important birthday, and that irritated her. She loved traditions because they do the thinking for you, simplifying life. In the end, she gave me the fur coat anyway, an old one of hers that had lost a lot of hairs, so she had had it mounted as a lining inside a raincoat. The note said, "To Isabella, don't worry, the minks died thirty years ago!"

THE SAGA OF THE FUR COAT AS TOLD BY MY MOTHER

"I found it difficult to fit into some Hollywood fashions. I never wanted a mink coat, and when I came to Hollywood and David Selznick saw that I didn't have one, he was absolutely flabbergasted; he couldn't believe it. Everybody had a mink coat! The fact that the climate makes a mink coat completely unnecessary has nothing to do with it. When you went to a party, it was the fashion to throw your coat into the lady's bedroom. The bed was piled high with mink; it groaned under mink coats.

"So when I was in New York one time, David telephoned Dan O'Shea to take me out and buy a mink coat. He didn't buy it; I had to pay for it myself. And I remember coming back to Hollywood and going to the next party, and as I threw my coat on top of all the other minks I felt disgusted. My mink wasn't half as nice as all the other minks; I still hadn't made it, my mink was too cheap because I just wouldn't buy *the* most expensive. So I sold it, and that was the end of that short story.

"David was very, very sad again, because he thought I hadn't attained the real status of a movie star in America. The following Christmas he kindly gave me a Persian lamb fur coat, which I liked much better, so that at least I owned a fur coat and didn't disgrace him.

"The same thing was repeated in Rome ten years later. Roberto Rossellini said in a shocked voice, 'Don't you have a mink coat?' And I said, 'No.' He said, 'But *every* woman has a mink coat. How come you didn't buy a mink coat? I mean, *everybody* in America has a mink coat.' And I said, 'Well, that's the reason I didn't want one. Everybody has a mink coat.' So what does he do? The following Christmas he gives me a mink coat. *That* mink coat I wore because it *wasn't* that usual in Italy. Not *everyone* had a mink coat. And because Roberto had given it to me. That mink coat I still have. It's doing its first really useful job. I've sewn it inside a raincoat. A warm, useful, mink-lined raincoat. Maybe eventually one of my daughters will like it."

Of my mother's three daughters, I was the one selected to receive for my twenty-first birthday the raincoat lined with mink. It still hangs in my closet. My children, horrified by the sight, propose to bury it in the pet cemetery we have in the country. That seems excessive.

My MOTHER IN THE FUR COAT

BUGS COPULATING IN MY YARD

One summer I took a really long vacation and decided to do something relaxing, like gardening. And then one day I noticed the roses, named after my mother, looking just awful: small flowers, wilted leaves, brown spots everywhere. Something was eating the Ingrid Bergman roses that were planted all around the perimeter of my garden. A close look at them, and I saw millions of small bugs hiding, disguising themselves in green to look like a stem or a leaf.

In my attempt to find out how to get rid of them, I lost my original plan, which was to garden in order to relax. The first pamphlet I read said something like "If you see ants along the stems of your plants"—which I did—"there must be aphids. It's the aphids that are affecting your plants, not the ants, which are just there to look after them. Aphids suck the sap from your plants . . ." and on it went, but my mind got stuck at that "look after them," and though I kept reading, "look after them" affected me the same way teachers had at school. An odd word, a strange sentence in a lesson would distract me from the lesson itself. "They ate meat: goats, sheep, pigs, dogs, cows . . ." Dogs!!! "The dead king was buried with his servants . . ." What? Buried with his servants? Were they dead or alive? And, if alive, what happened? Were there screams, protests, or did they just peacefully accept their fate? Given sentences like those, I would no longer follow the essential teachings of the lessons: the wars, the political complexities, the discoveries. School was terribly distracting to me, and that "look after them" was, too. So my mother's roses all died—eaten up by the aphids—and I got involved in the life of bugs and stopped relaxing with gardening.

This is what I found out: aphids are all female. The only difference among them is that some have wings and fly away to eat other people's gardens and some are wingless and stay to keep eating yours. Aphids give birth to female babies, which give birth to other females, repeating over and over again that extraordinary method of virginal reproduction.

In the winter, though, with the cold weather, they give birth to male babies in the more conventional way. These are born without mouths and never eat, they are just sex machines. They mate and they mate, and the females give birth to eggs this time, not baby females. These eggs will hatch only the following spring and give birth to females once again, and then on for another season.

The ants "look after" aphids because the aphids are their . . . cows. Now, the scientific books I read did not say it in those exact words, but this is what they mean and what I understood. By stroking the aphids' bellies, like milking them, the ants make the aphids release honeydew, which they eat. Ants look after aphids the way cowboys do their herds. For example, during bad weather, they gather them up and push them into their nests until the sun comes back, or they collect their eggs and carry them into the underground chambers of their nests until the following spring, when they place them back out in a nearby plant so that when the aphids hatch out of the eggs, they can be comfortably milked. The ants' regimented and military social organization provides the aphids with protection from predators. Apparently, beetles and lacewings want to eat them and aphids have only a poor system of protection: farting. They fart out a yellow wax in the face of their enemy, and that's that. But they don't only risk being eaten. Wasps—pregnant wasps—lay eggs inside other creatures' bodies before their ferocious and carnivorous larvae are born, because, if left in their mother's uterus, the babies will start eating their mother from within. If you see a bug or an aphid, no more bright, beautiful, Ingrid Bergman green but brownish black and looking funny and different from the others, you can be sure there is a larva inside it at work. Once the baby wasps are ready to come out, they cut a hole through the aphid's body the way we open a tin can with a can opener.

Well, can you understand that when I found all this out I wanted to know more? I looked for bugs in my garden, I identified the species and read more about them in books. It became an obsession, and that's how I lost relaxing that summer.

Do you remember when we were children, we were taught to praise the bees for their relentless work of collecting and storing food for the winter? All to suggest to us to be careful with money, save for old age, disease, and disaster, have bank accounts, savings accounts, bonds, and so on. And we were told that cicadas just sing all the time—"Tra-la-la-la, tra-la-la-la"—and die with the first cold weather, because they spend the summer doing nothing. Right? Were you told these stories, too? That was to discourage us from living a fast life, burning out having fun, and dying young.

Well, what they didn't tell us is that bees are incestuous. Okay, they work, but the future queen is fucked by one of her brothers! Once his penis penetrates her vagina and does its thing, it breaks off. The poor brother bleeds to death, and the sister uses the broken organ as a plug to prevent the semen from running out of her and also as a chastity belt to prevent other males from mating with her. As for cicadas, they don't have a brief life at all. They live underground in the soil for years as nymphs, which means that they look different, but it's the same animal. They come out of the ground years later just to mate.

Their singing is a serenade, males calling to females by rubbing their forewings together in song.

Think for a moment what frightening, strange faces insects have when you look at them closely or under a microscope. Can you imagine what their reproductive organs would look like?

Do you know the vagina is considered to be a very old organ, which has been around since the beginning of time, but the penis is considered an evolved organ that belongs only to more sophisticated animals?

Take an earthworm. It's not considered very evolved. What it has doesn't even deserve to be called a "penis," it's simply referred to as the "seminal vesicle." It's a pathetic little attribute that shares only one thing with a penis—it's masculine, but that's as far as it goes. Earthworms are hermaphrodites—male and female at the same time all in one animal. They copulate, though, not with themselves but with another earthworm in a position we call "69"—the head of one touching the tail of the other.

The female of another type of worm performs the biggest oral sex ever: she swallows her mate.

In yet other species of worms the males don't even have to bother being born. They copulate with their sisters while still inside the womb.

Spiders have to practice a kind of masturbation on whatever little attribute they have between their legs. They collect the sperm with a pair of their hands and insert it, one fistful at a time, into the female's vagina.

The worm Maria Callas allegedly swallowed to lose eighty pounds, the tapeworm, practices incest. It has a system of male and female organs, and it introduces its own penis into its own vagina. When I worked with Steven Meisel doing a story on

Callas for *Allure* magazine, we played her records, listened to her magnificent voice, and thought and talked a lot about what was taking place in the great diva's intestines.

I saw a snail penis. It's a hard white thing, though I'm not sure . . . it might also be the kind of dildo they use for sexual stimulation. Raised up belly to belly or foot to foot (since their belly is also their foot), two snails rock back and forth until one of them injects its "dildo" into its partner's body, stimulating sexual excitement. The other snail, pained, strikes back. This provokes the erection of their penises, which apparently are enormous (they certainly are if they're that white thing I saw). Each snail's penis is pushed deep into the other's vagina. Every snail has a penis and a vagina, so that four sex organs are involved in copulation.

I read about a snail that changes gender. The young snails are all male, but they become female after copulating. The transsexual transformation occurs when the male is still attached to the female, attracting a third snail, a male, which attaches itself to the first two and, after ejaculation, starts transforming into a female. This attracts a fourth male and a fifth, building up a sexual tower of ten, fourteen snails with the females at one end, the males at the other, and all the different degrees of males changing into females in the middle.

SEX

With all that—masturbation, group sex, sadism, incest, sexual suicide, cannibalism, and so on—we get to the eternal life. A scientific book states, "The eternal life might be achieved only by the species, individual after individual. All living individuals are mortal. . . ." I do not like that. For science, the real essence of me is contained in the eggs that crowd in my ovaries and are shed month after month before my period. Isn't that a horrifying way to describe me?

Not that I love the more common "You look so sexy" kind of remark, either. I don't like it. At a "You-look-sexy" I generally smile and thank, diplomat that I am, but secretly I feel offended by it. When I took my clothes off in *Blue Velvet*, I wanted to convey the brutality of sex abuse. I wanted to look like a quartered cow hanging in a butcher shop as well as disturbingly appealing.

When the film came out, I was told by some that I had looked sexy and played a great femme fatale. Others told me I should have insisted on being photographed in a more flattering way. All that made me feel I'd failed at portraying the reality of abused women, the many layers, the horrible twists, the unclear emotions. Of all my work, only *Blue Velvet* offered me the opportunity to show the complexity of sex.

Sex is an interesting subject to investigate because it incorporates both the highest and the lowest aspects of life, from the most loving to the most abusive, the lightest to the darkest, and all the shades in between. That's why I agreed to work with Madonna and Steven Meisel on their book, *Sex*. At first I declined: "I've got kids. I can't risk losing my Lancôme contract, as I learned from *Blue Velvet*." Madonna and Steven insisted, and they sounded so interesting in their search to understand and illustrate all the varieties and shades sex could take. "I don't want to appear nude or French-kiss you, Madonna." "Okay," she answered, and off we went to Miami for the photos. We dressed up like men, playing around like girlfriends making fun of boys. When the photos came out, in the context of the book, it looked as if we were lesbians. Lancôme got upset, but it was easy to defend myself: "What's the matter with being a lesbian?" That deflected any proceedings against me.

While I was married to Martin, my first *Vogue* cover appeared. Martin refused to go out all that month—March 1982. "How can you think I'd be happy seeing people, strangers, looking with lust and desire at your photo hanging on all the street kiosks?" he would ask me. I found his reaction utterly charming.

When years later I was told by a proud agent, smiling at me, that Gary Oldman, whom I was involved with at the time, had finally become a sex symbol in Hollywood, I reacted much like Martin. I wanted to fumigate the house, starting with the mattress of the bed we shared. It didn't make me proud that he had chosen me. It didn't give a kick to my ego to know I was envied by others. I kept my eyes closed through most of his films anyway, love scenes first. And I didn't like to see him killed, either. One or the other and most likely both were apt to happen in all his work. I didn't watch Gary's films; I listened to them, as if they were radio programs.

The same goes for Martin's films and all those bloody scenes he always has. I find them too hard to watch. I close my eyes. Yet I once saw Martin pass out at the sight of his own blood. Just a drop of it, and he passed out. It was at the doctor's, and his finger was being pricked to collect a sample for medical analysis. When he was revived, I shouted at him, "See what you do to the rest of us?" I meant with his films.

INGRID

Ingrid, my twin sister, with whom I share no telepathic experiences such as other twins have, called me a few days ago from a

library. Excitement was pushing words out of her mouth so fast I had to ask her several times to repeat herself. " 'Cosmetic' comes from *kosmos*. The word 'cosmetic' has something to do with the universe. I am so glad," she blurted, and then she hung up. "Glad about what?" I asked myself, but I knew.

My twin sister, Ingrid, and me

She is a Ph.D. professor of medieval literature, and she has to find ways of redeeming and understanding what it is about cosmetics and fashion—even film, for that matter—that grips me. The first time I agreed to be in a film, she commented, "What courage!" as if I had volunteered to go to war. On a rare occasion when she joined me at a dinner party at Bruce Weber's, she dragged me out as soon as the other guests arrived. "Those are real models. We'd better leave." She was afraid that standing there face to face with real beauties I was going to be unmasked. Everybody would see I was an impostor.

Our lives are so different that if Ingrid weren't my sister chances are we would never have met. But since we're twins, we know each other better than any other human being. We know how to give each other a heartthrob or a palpitation. I wouldn't know how to do it to others with the same precision I can aim at Ingrid's heart. A while ago I placed a paper napkin from a Paris café in an envelope and sent it to her. I knew that when she saw the little logo in the corner of the napkin, it would send her right back into early childhood. She did notice the little sign, and it did send her into a memory trip. Once I wrapped up a one-inch blue tile and gave it to her for Christmas. I knew the association with this little tile would trigger happy feelings in her. She still treasures it, keeping it, in fact, in a jewelry box with the aquamarines, the pearls, and the rubies Dad gave her when he came back from India.

" 'Cosmetic' comes from the Greek *kosmos,* which means 'order of the universe,' " Ingrid faxed me in a typed note so there wasn't any risk of my misunderstanding the great discovery words. " 'Order' in Greek is also the word for 'adorn' and 'embellish.' " And this is how, to my twin's great relief, cosmetics came to be associated with something of value: the cosmos. My family reads etymological entries in dictionaries the way others read tarot cards or the *I Ching*.

"You don't have to go to school," my dad declared. " 'To educate' comes from the verb 'to castrate.' If you go to the source of the words, you find out the true nature of things." With this in mind, I dropped out of high school. But years later, my sister Ingrid announced to me that "to educate" comes from the root *duc,* which derives from the Latin *dux* or *ducis,* which means "leader." Remember how Mussolini referred to himself? As "Il Duce." The etymological meaning of "to educate" is "to lead," with derivations that extend to words such as "seduce" because it brings to you, it attracts to you. "But I found nothing that links 'educate' to 'castrate,' " she told me, dispirited. She knows how, for thirty years, I made "educate equals castrate" my shield against my shame and embarrassment over being a school dropout.

"Do you mean Father was wrong? Where did he get it? Maybe the word wasn't 'educate' but 'learn' or 'teach.' Check it out, Ingrid." But "learn" in Italian—*imparare*—comes from the Latin *parens* ("parent"), which leads to Italian words such as *partorire* ("to give birth") and then, via leaps I couldn't follow despite Ingrid's attempts to explain them, to the verb "appropriate." To learn is to possess—but no reference to castration. And "to teach"—another disappointment. *Insegnare,* Italian for "to teach," comes from the Latin *signum,* which means "brand" or "sign of distinction" and from which is derived the English word "signature." But here, too, no echo of castration. Ingrid is the only person on earth who would know what a blow this is to me. I feel stripped and exposed to what a school dropout really is: an ignorant person just like me.

I shared everything with Ingrid—not only a bedroom, bathroom, and clothes but even school—until I was thirteen. That's when I got sick, missed a year of school, and found myself the following year in a class full of young girls I considered snotty, and no longer with Ingrid. I endured school for two more years and then dropped out with that cocky slogan in my head: "To educate is to castrate."

That etymological "finding" of my father's was exactly how school made me feel—diminished, oppressed, reduced. The mere sitting at a desk for so many consecutive hours, restraining my physical movements, made me feel I was going to suffocate. It took all I had just to sit still; nothing was left in me to follow the lessons. Ingrid knew how little I knew. The moment my name was called out by a teacher to answer any question, Ingrid would inevitably start to cry. Accompanied by this sisterly Greek chorus of lament, I would set about the humiliating process of exposing my ignorance publicly. Homework, exams, and papers were easier: I would copy Ingrid's. Consequently, when she moved on to a higher grade that aspect of my schooling collapsed as well.

You may not know how hippopotamuses defecate. I had forgotten about it until I read *The Jungle Book* by Kipling, who, by the way, I thought was a relative of mine,

began my written assignment on this book.

When I was six years old, my father left for one of his fabulous trips. He came back two years later with a beautiful Indian wife with a red dot in her forehead and a new brother and sister for me, Gil and Raffaella. During his absence he wrote to me often. He sent letters with drawings of the globe and maps to explain to me where India is, or telegrams: "It's hot. Love—Papa" or "Today it's 103 degrees. Love—Papa." Once he sent a photo of himself riding an elephant. My mother, during his absence, told me about Mowgli, Bagheera the panther, and Kaa the python. It was the first time I'd heard about them. I don't know how, but in my mind my mother's tale and my father's trip overlapped and mixed and I ended up assuming Kipling was a member of my new Indian family. When my father came back, he had fabulous stories to tell me. One of them was about how hippopotamuses defecate. They come out of the water and shake their tails fast back and forth splashing feces all about. An African legend explains why the hippo defecates in this unusual way. It is an African legend not an Indian one, but when I was six and heard this story I didn't know the difference. The hippo was the last animal God created. He had used all the legs, tails, eyes, ears He had available. He put together the hippo with whatever was left. The result was this strange-looking creature who was too big. God worried that if the hippo came to live on earth it would have to eat so much it would endanger the survival of other species who lived in water. The hippo wanted very much to become alive. It promised God it would never eat any fish but only grass. Still today, when it has to defecate, it comes out of the water and with its tail breaks up the feces to show God it kept its promise.

I wrote reports that were so made up I hoped to deflect the teacher's attention from the fact that I hadn't really studied. I would use what had distracted me in the first place—fantasy— to distract. Fantasy, I planned, would be my weapon, but this technique was never very effective with my teachers. They would quickly unmask me: "You didn't follow the assignment. Instead of studying, you just used your imagination. You don't need school for that."

DEFORMITY

When I was eleven years old, I was diagnosed with scoliosis. I stood naked except for my underwear in a long queue of girls in the school gym. A doctor was to examine all of us and decide if we were fit to do physical education. Before that, the only exercise we had done in school was marching, just like little soldiers.

"Tell your parents you are not to take this class. You have scoliosis, a deformity of the spine." If I have a deformity, it means I am deformed, I thought, and the news crushed me. I was indeed to become deformed in the two years my condition worsened and as we desperately looked for a cure. Hanging by my neck for hours every day did not help, nor did the special gymnastics with which I was to develop muscles on one side or the other of my back to force the curvature of my spine to straighten up.

Scoliosis is a rotation of the vertebrae that results in twisting of the spine, which pushes the rib cage, the hips, everything out of line. As my spine was bending more and more into an "S" shape, I limped slightly and one scapula stood out. To make it acceptable, it was referred to as "Isabella's wing," but that definition failed to console me. Later on, I saw a severe case of scoliosis—a young girl's torso so twisted she looked like a little ball in her bed, her lungs so compressed that her breath was too shallow to blow out a lighted match.

It was Professor Alberto Ponte who helped me with my condition. Thirty years later, he was to diagnose a scoliosis in Elettra that she inherited from me. He is now helping her with a whole new treatment that is less complex and painful than what I had to endure.

To correct my scoliosis, I was attached to a special machine by the neck and the hips and pulled in opposite directions. Once the maximum correction was obtained, I was put into a cast. A few weeks later, after my body had given in to that stretch, skin and veins elongated, I was stretched a little more and wrapped in another cast. This was all done while I was awake, without painkillers, because the "maximum correction" that can be obtained depends on how much pain a patient can endure—the stretching stopped when I passed out. The cast went from my hips all the way up to my neck and the back of my head. The pressure of the cast made my bite so tight that my teeth could have been pushed back into the jawbone. For that, I had to have a special brace to keep my teeth in order. After four months of this treatment, my S-shaped spine was corrected and fixed straight with an operation that consisted of a bone transplant taken from my leg. Thirteen of my vertebrae were fused together. After this operation, I had to stay in bed for six months with a cast on my torso to restrict all movement and allow the bones to fuse together, and a cast on my leg to allow the bone to grow back. I was then allowed to stand up, but, still wearing the cast on my torso, I had to relearn how to walk. Six months after that, when the last cast was removed, my head hung from my neck like a choked chicken until I reeducated those muscles as well.

My mother was very worried and disturbed by my illness. She gave up work and stayed with me until I got well, two years later. I was moved by her decision and felt guilty about taking her away from what she loved so much—acting. Maybe it was then that I learned one can wish for opposite things that can never be reconciled: I wanted my mother to be with me, but at the same time I wanted her not to give up working on account of me. The resolution to never, ever be a weight on anybody's life again gave me the determination and strong drive to become independent. And I did.

My mother wrote about my scoliosis in her autobiography. That flattered me. The one good thing that comes from disease, disgrace, and sorrow is the sympathy you elicit. I still remember the day I pretended to be asleep on the couch in the living room but was really listening to my mother warn my brother and sisters to be particularly good and understanding with me: "She's going through a very hard time." That gave me a warm sensation and a confirmation that maybe I was indeed living something out of the ordinary, something exceptional. Was this an opportunity rather than a setback toward that full and interesting life I'd promised myself to live?

The hardest aspect of being ill is the physical pain. I had no remedies for pain, but I learned to "go marble" to endure it. "Go marble" is the name I gave it; it was a kind of checking out of my own body, as if it didn't belong to me. "Me" was just my thoughts; my body was an appendage of mine I could ignore. I used it when I was raped and when I got beaten up. Years later, an American soldier who had been a prisoner in the Korean War described to me what he had done to endure his imprisonment. It sounded like "going marble."

Obviously I am proud of being a model—it's a great feeling of having conquered the odds—from deformed to "one of the most beautiful women in the world," as I am sometimes described. "Don't be modest, just say it . . . come on . . . *often* described," one of my voices from the beyond, maybe my mother or an aunt, encourages me to say. So, let me phrase it again: It's a great feeling of having conquered the odds—from deformed to "one of the most beautiful women in the world," as I am *often* described. I have often felt reluctant to talk a lot about my illness, because great wisdom is expected to come out of disease, disgrace, and pain, and I don't think I got any wisdom out of my scoliosis. When asked in interviews, "What is the lesson you learned in your two years of illness?" I would answer, "That health is the most important thing. I am grateful every day to walk, to see, to talk." But this answer, though it is absolutely true and correct, seems made for the kind of trash journalism that promotes trash wisdom and trash culture, that goes with trash music and trash food, and I have blushed every time I've used it. Mostly, my illness gave me an orgy of emotions that, especially at the beginning, I didn't know how to organize and give meaning to.

For years, I couldn't go to a hospital, smell a medicine cabinet, visit a sick friend. I didn't feel anything other than an obstinate, powerful refusal even to come close to pain, illness, or sadness. I felt compassion and understanding for people who suffered, but mostly just terror, and this made me guilty and weak. With time the terror of the hospital and the illness subsided.

The gravity of what I had lived through became clear to me only when my daughter got sick. For some inexplicable reason I always find it hard to admit and recognize that hardships happen to me. I recognize them when they happen to others but belittle them when it's my turn because for me making demands on others is the most painful admission—the one I fear weighs now on the sweet heart of my teenage daughter. She, like me, always wants to please, to be no bother or worry to anybody.

Happiness, as my mother pointed out, might be good health and a short memory, but what to do with the genetic memory, which is inescapable? I hope the illness I have passed on will not make my daughter and all our descendants come to feel cursed. I hope that since it affects a lot of us, it will make us feel less alone with it.

ADOPTION

QUESTION: HOW DOES IT FEEL TO LOOK AT YOUR CHILD, KNOWING THAT NOTHING OF YOUR PARENTS, WHOM THE ENTIRE WORLD ADORED, IS IN THAT BABY?

ANSWER: THE GENETIC CONNECTION IN ADOPTION INCLUDES MY PARENTS AND GOES FAR BEYOND THEM, ALL THE WAY BACK TO ADAM AND EVE.

That's what popped out of my mouth, and it surprised me. I thought the question was cruel and thoughtless and I was hurt by it, but my answer struck me. For a moment I feared I was going to be laughed at. Was there something about bringing in Adam and Eve to explain the composition of my family that made my answer too apocalyptic? If I had given it due thought, I don't know what I would have answered—either something to strike back at the insensitive interlocutor or some rational, articulate, patient, and probably overly long explanation about genes, chromosomes, and what really makes a family. But my answer got blurted out, the way truth does.

Adoption feels like genetic connection because it links you directly not only to your own gene pool but to the genes of all humanity, all the way to the roots from which we all originated. It feels as if my hand has stretched past my immediate family and, by reaching out, found more kindred others. In comparison to having a biological child—I have one of those, too—adoption carries the added dimension of connection not only to your own tribe but beyond, widening the scope of what constitutes love, ties, and family. It is a larger embrace. This "larger embrace" was a surprise to me. I didn't expect it because in most cases the decision to adopt starts as a remedy—for not having one's own children or for not having as many children as one would like. It's a remedy for the family one has dreamed of having but didn't get. And "remedy" carries the idea of "less than." Instead, it was as if I fell into an unexpected river of abundance, love, connection, union, belonging.

The feeling of "larger embrace" that adopting gave me extended not only to Roberto but also to his family of origin: his birth mother, birth father, birth grandparents, as they are referred to. I don't remember what I thought and imagined about birth mothers and birth fathers before adopting, while I was still in the process of making the decision. I don't think I thought of much beyond the endless debate in my head about the issue of adopting as a single mother. Hasn't every child, after all, the right to both a father and mother? Would I ever be able to give the baby a real sense of family without a father at home? But the more I thought about these questions, the more they seemed to belong to the kind of wisdom that states "It is better to be born beautiful and rich than ugly and poor." I was wishing for another baby and knowing that out there there was a baby wishing to have a home. Adopting meant that a baby who would otherwise have "no one" would at least have me. But "no one" turned out to be a devastatingly moving reality, so devastatingly moving that it's often not spoken about and birth parents are relegated to silence and being forgotten.

Before starting the process of adoption, I still had what I now refer to as "the Oliver Twist romantic notion" of it. I imagined abandoned babies, abandoned for many reasons: from perverted mothers who just didn't care to women who thought of abortion as a crime, from drug addiction to social shame. "Abandoned" was the word I had in mind when thinking about adoption. But in Roberto's case there was no abandonment. Whatever notion lingered in me that I was going to save a baby from being abandoned was torn away. My vanity and vague self-congratulatory feelings were immediately put into their places.

Instead, the power of my privilege became clearer. I could do what many birth mothers could not: both financially and emotionally, I could afford to have a child, even as a single mother. I would not be excommunicated from my social milieu, I would not lose my job, I would not be thrown out of my family, and, most of all, I would have the absolute certitude that I will be able to feed and school this child until he is an adult. Adoption took me from the pedestal of my social privileges and bonded me with the realities I'd only heard about until then but had not belonged to. Adoption connected me to other worlds and other realities. It's the "larger embrace" effect again, so that when I'm told "How lucky for Roberto to have been adopted," I feel, in fact, that I'm the lucky one. I wanted a baby, and I ended up with so much more. Roberto brought with him a sense of communion that breached class, cultural, and social divisions.

The bridge that I didn't need Roberto to help me build was the bond and solidarity among all of us women. We have a lot to share, including the secret terror of staring at our unstained underwear, waiting for our period and fearing an undesired pregnancy. The consequences of a pregnancy are dramatic and drastic: abortion, adoption, foster care, or mothering. For women, there is no escape.

"You're in touch with the birth mother! What if she shows up on your doorstep someday?" I am asked with great apprehension. Well, what if she does? Why would it necessarily be an antagonistic relationship? Adoption, with its "larger embrace" effect, has helped me every day with the need to practice decency, caring, and tenderness. Letting the birth mother know that Roberto is loved, cared for, and all right can only lessen the chances of anxiety, remorse, and sorrow. Don't I owe that to my son's birth mother? Isn't it the greatest gift for Roberto to know that instead of abandonment and neglect there is love and care, that instead of shame there is now dignity, that instead of secrecy there is now friendship?

"Aren't you afraid that she'll want him back or that he'll want to be her son and not yours?" Both those things will happen. She will have those feelings, Roberto will have those feelings, and the three of us will have to live with that. The stakes are high, but aren't they always with anyone we love so much that our own happiness depends on him?

"Model/actress Isabella Rossellini, daughter of Ingrid Bergman and Roberto Rossellini, caught walking down the street with her daughter, Elettra, and her adopted son, Roberto." That is how the paparazzi photos taken of me and my children are invariably captioned. That "adopted son" isn't really there to inform the reader. I worry about Roberto. Will his feelings be hurt by the bigotry still surrounding adoption? It hurts me. Once, when I introduced my children to a woman, she asked me, "Which one is the real one?" I gasped and consoled myself by reminding myself that she was uninformed, that she will learn, and that if she gets to know us she will understand.

It was reported to me that some people leaving a party were overheard saying, "Isabella doesn't know what she's doing. She's brought into her home the street problem and racial conflict. Her daughter will suffer from it." But I myself am the daughter of a mixed-race family, and I haven't suffered from it. I have always thought it was a privilege. I have mixed in me the very north and the very south of Europe, Scandinavian and Mediterranean blood. My mother was half German, half Swedish. My sister Raffaella is half Italian and half Indian, and Gil, who genetically is all Indian, was adopted by my father. There is Alessandro, my nephew, my eldest brother's son and the one who made my dad a grandfather for the first time, whose mother is a black American. Now there are also Renzo's younger children, who are part Jewish. There is still more blood—Irish and Russian. If you were to see all of us in a row, you'd never guess we're all one family. Growing up, this made me feel our family was very avant-garde, evolved, and ahead of the others still struggling with the prejudice of racial differences.

Our lives were also enriched by everybody's traditions, the strongest being Italian, Indian, Swedish, American, and French.

None of us can in reality claim a genetic connection to France, but that's the country in which most of us have lived at least a part of our lives, and, to me, Paris is my city more than Stockholm is.

When I had to write on the numerous adoption papers whether I had a preference for any race, I wrote: "Anything, preferably non-white." I do not consider myself white. I wanted my family to carry on as it already was—mixed. I don't feel my Swedish blood washed away everything else. In America, people refer to South Americans as "Latinos." In Europe, "Latin people" are all those whose languages are based on Latin: Spanish, Portuguese, French, Italian, and Romanian. It took me some time to understand that in America I couldn't claim to be a "Latino," even though my genes come from Mediterranean ancestors like those of the *conquistadores* of the Americas. Anyway, "Latino" is not a race per se, but a name for a prejudice.

I don't feel I have chosen my children but rather that they were destined to me. I don't feel I have chosen Roberto because, since he is my adopted son, I had that opportunity, just as I don't feel I have chosen Elettra because, since she is my biological daughter, I passed on to her both my genes and her daddy's. Actually, what makes family to me is a sense of destiny. I did not choose my parents or my siblings. I was destined to be Ingrid and Roberto's daughter and the sister of Romano, Renzo, Pia, Roberto, Ingrid, Gil, and Raffaella. They are my family, whether I like it or not. The inexorability of this fate that defines family extends, for me, to my children. Elettra has brown eyes. Since she is blond and very fair, we all expected her to have blue eyes. Jonathan, his mother, Flo, and his father, Fred, all have blue eyes. Mine are hazel, my mother's blue, but my dad . . . he had brown eyes, and that's what Elettra got. Roberto, although partly African American, has blue eyes. I jokingly say, "My black baby is turning Swedish." To me, the randomness of it all is what makes it miraculous and romantic. I wish I could claim both Roberto and Elettra as brilliant and wise decisions of mine. But the two of them are not my "choices," they are my children.

A WILL AND TOMBS

For years I did not want to draw up a will because I feared it would bring me bad luck. The mere act of signing that document, I thought, could kill me. But reason got the better of me. Not only the responsibility toward my children, but also an unexpected and sudden turn of my superstition. I knew that when things are said out loud, you can expect the opposite to happen. While working on a film, if someone predicts, "This is going to be a success," you know it won't be. That statement alone could kill all its chances. Maybe the same could happen with my will, I thought. Drawing it up and signing it will not make me die sooner, it will probably prolong my life.

So I went to my lawyer and started the process. Then I became enthusiastic over it. There are so many ways of leaving your money, even to people who don't yet exist. The laws allow your not-yet-born descendants to be your heirs. I became enthralled with leaving something to everybody: old friends, new friends, existing and nonexisting family members (in America, you can set up trusts for grandchildren yet to be born!), employers and employees, even nice people I hadn't had enough time to become close friends with—it became like Christmas, like shopping and trying to figure out how to please and surprise everyone. It took me weeks to complete the draft of my will, and once I had done it I felt like sitting down and waiting for the event to take place. I was so looking forward to my friends' reactions. Then I caught myself. I made a lot of corna

and that helped me come to another realization: If I wasn't going to be the one to wish for my death, my friends would—just out of curiosity to see what I had left them. What would that do to my life span? I started to wonder. I decided to tell no one about my will, my intentions, not even what my estate consisted of. I opted for a kind of *omertà*—the thick, impenetrable silence of Mafia victims who do not collaborate with police. Around my will, *omertà* is what's called for, I decided. So I will say no more about it, except for one last detail of which I'm proud.

In my will I left instructions on how and where I want to be buried. That takes guts, you know. Not even Anna Magnani, the toughest, most earthy woman in the history of cinema, had the guts to buy herself a tomb. She ended up, in fact, in our family tomb at the Pincetto in Verano until Luca, her son, made a more permanent arrangement for her.

People envied our Pincetto tomb. It was Nonno Zeffiro (my great-grandfather, friend of Garibaldi) who made the arrangements for us in this very elegant spot of the ancient cemetery in Rome. The arrangement is in perpetuity, my family assures me, though I fear that "in perpetuity" is going to be shorter than that. In legal language, "in perpetuity"—is it ten years? two hundred years? or truly forever? One of these days I will not be surprised if we are all thrown out—rotten coffins, bones, and all. Meanwhile, people think that our chapel at Pincetto is truly enviable, a sign of great distinction, the one glory unanimously attributed to us Rossellinis.

Nuzza, our baby-sitter when we were children, looked for a spot for herself at Verano, not to be close to us but for the status a tomb at Pincetto can give. She chose an available *fornetto,* a spot in the thick wall of dead bodies that goes up five rows. With a big ladder like the ones in old libraries that runs along the wall, even the dead up high can receive visits from loved ones and flowers can be left in appropriate receptacles. Nuzza chose her *fornetto* next to a doctor's and a lawyer's: "Professionals, not just anyone," she told me proudly, making a face of disdain when she pronounced the word "anyone." I knew whom she meant: the unemployed, thieves, good-for-nothings like some of my parents' friends whom she judged to be just leeches, hangers-on who were taking advantage of *la Signora,* as she referred to Mother, and *il Dottore,* as she referred to Father. She chose the side of the wall of corpses that received some sun a few hours each day because, she explained, it made her feel that it would make being buried "not as depressing as it could be." She was also pleased to see that the lawyer's tomb always had fresh flowers. One time we ran into the widow who was taking such good care of it. "Don't forget me, madam. Bring a little flower for me too when my time comes, because if I wait for the Rossellinis to bring me anything, forget it. Not even the children"—and that included me—"will bring a twig, after all I've done for them." "Nuzza, stop it, stop it. It's not true. I will love you forever," I would protest, but deep down I knew she was right. I know in my heart I will not visit her tomb—maybe once, yes—but that will be it. She's not dead yet, and already I neglect calling her. She lives in Sardinia, and no matter how many times I have told her I would visit, I never have.

Nuzza taught me not to be afraid of the dead. She used that efficient technique that is not the mere spoken word—an intellectual activity that has proven over and over not to be effective with me—but the actual physical experience of it that makes it a lesson unforgettable and indelible. One day she deliberately lingered in the cemetery after dusk, when the gate closed. When my anxiety rose to near panic, she declared, "Never fear the dead ones, who can hurt no one; rather, fear the alive ones." With that she gave me the first necessary help in overcoming my horror and terror of tombs, corpses, funerals, and cemeteries. I now love to spend a day at the cemetery cleaning tombs. It is a great family-bonding experience—more powerful than birthday parties, which I always celebrate with great pomp. I go to the cemetery with a basketful of flowers, Ajax, sponges, Windex, and bug powder. You know those ants—they'll eat anything. I always have to leave a thin row of white poison powder around all the coffins.

It was on one of those visits to clean the tombs that Zia Marcella, who accompanied me, said something about Anna Magnani that became a revelation of her personality. I had never really known Anna Magnani, though at home she was considered a sort of distant relative or a close friend, that kind of category. Daddy took me to see her only once. I was very nervous; not only was she a famous star, but my mommy had stolen my dad away from her. She had been really hurt and upset about it—she had thrown the famous bowl of spaghetti over my dad's head. That story is in all the biographies: Mother's, Father's,

Anna's. I even read it in an essay on Italian cinema. Do you know the story? I will repeat it.

Father was about to film *Stromboli,* the first film he did with Mother. Mother had written him a letter telling him she wanted to work with him, and with her customary belief that speaking languages could open any professional door, she specified, "I speak Swedish, German, English, French, but in Italian I only know how to say *'ti amo'* [I love you]." She didn't mean it the way the myth of my parents' love tells it; those really were her only two words in Italian. She wrote to him because she admired his films and wished to work with him. Dad, though, was quite taken by having impressed the biggest star in Hollywood. He liked her. Anna was not happy. Anna and Daddy were spending a weekend at the Hotel Luna in Amalfi. Daddy told the concierge he was expecting a telegram from Los Angeles and to please give it to him privately, not in front of Anna Magnani. But the stupid concierge, as Father and Anna passed him in the hall on their way to the restaurant, winked at Dad. Anna got it and got it all. Sitting at the table, they ordered pasta. Pleasantly she asked, "Roberto, do you want more sauce? A bit more olive oil? Some parmigiano?" She tossed the spaghetti, and when it was all ready to be eaten, she poured the contents over Father's head. That was the beginning of the end of their relationship . . . or maybe it was the end, the final act, I don't remember any longer, and I've heard this story so many times I never want to hear it again. Whatever it was, just know that a little later, after Father and Anna split, Mother and Father worked together, fell in love, got married, and we were born . . . not quite in that order. It was a bit more messy than that, but all of the above did indeed happen.

When Dad took me to see Anna that one time, I was scared.

I had seen her in films—strong, foul-mouthed, ready to curse, slapping men right and left. I worried that she would hate me after what Mamma had done to her. I kept my eyes lowered throughout the visit and didn't say a word and prayed for Dad to make it a quick visit and get out of her apartment. With my eyes lowered, I saw nothing of Anna's house decor or her personal style of clothing, just her feet. She wore satin slippers with a little heel—very feminine and out of character, I thought—and many pets roamed around her feet. They were mostly cats—some beautiful with thick, Persian fur, others rickety and miserable that she must have collected in the street, and some that seemed the result of too-heavy interbreeding that was probably taking place right there in the confines of her apartment. In a corner, lying on a blanket, a dog that looked like the Big Bad Wolf of "Little Red Riding-Hood" growled at me anytime I looked at her. I recognized the dog: it was Micia, Anna and Dad's pet when they had been together. I recognized her because I had gotten a glimpse of her in their film version of "The Human Voice," Jean Cocteau's monologue. But that dog must have been dead by then. What I saw, I fear, was its ghost. Although Anna may have reached down with her hand and pinched my cheek the way grown-ups do to show children affection, her dog from the beyond growled to remind me of other feelings present in that room, even if Anna wasn't showing them. The faithful Micia hadn't forgiven all the sorrow her mistress had suffered because of my mom and dad.

That's all I had in the way of direct contact and experience with Anna Magnani. My family referred to her only as a great actress—my mother, too, admired her tremendously—but nothing personal was ever said about Anna until the day Zia Marcella, looking at the coffin taking up so much room in the chapel, said,

"She was a pushy person alive, she's a pushy person dead."

"Zia . . . Zia Anna . . . my dear, dear aunt . . ." wailed my cousin Franco at the screen during the retrospective of Anna Magnani's films at the Museum of Modern Art in New York many years after her death. Franco made me so embarrassed I froze in my seat. He claimed and exaggerated any relationship to famous people. He was the only person who requested that his obituary end with a list not only of those who survived him but also those who had died before him. It read, "Pre-deceased by his aunt, Ingrid Bergman." In my seat at the screening room of MoMA, I couldn't move or stand, I could hardly blink, I could barely breathe. I think I experienced a kind of an alive "rigor mortis." Franco gave me that sensation several times when he was alive and once even after his death.

Franco wailed his "Arab widow kind of lament" again at the screening of *Joan of Arc at the Stake,* the lost-and-found-again film of the oratorio by Paul Claudel and Arthur Honegger that my mother did, directed by my father. The film had been lost for nearly twenty-five years until it was discovered on a shelf in a film lab in Turin, restored by the Italian government, and shown at the Cannes Film Festival. The press waited for me and my brother to emerge from the screening room with comments. I knew they hoped to capture a few tears in our eyes, and indeed we were moved. But Franco followed us, and, placing himself directly behind us, his head between ours so that the camera couldn't miss him, began his wailing lament: "Zia Ingrid . . . Zio Roberto . . ." complete with tears, snot, handkerchief, hands on his head, and a fainting spell. Both Roberto and I fell into the "rigor mortis" of embarrassment that Franco was so capable of provoking in us. When we saw ourselves on the TV news that evening, we seemed cold and stiff, giving monosyllabic grunts for answers like something out of a horror movie. In fact, we looked like proof of the belief that children of geniuses and stars are stupid, neurotic, cold, spoiled, and snobbish.

But it was Franco's fault. He loved to create chaos, he was a horror that way. My little daughter, Elettra, stressed out by Franco's constant teasing, mockery, and kidnapping of her beloved dog, Macaroni, asked me, "Is Franco truly your first cousin? Is there any way you can make him your last?"

On Franco's deathbed, a priest came to give him the last rites. The temptation to commit a final mischievous act gave him renewed energy. "I want to confess," he declared, finding the strongest voice he had had in days. I looked at him and then at the poor priest. Already Franco was asking, "Are you a Dominican? You know Monsignor So-and-So? I had an affair with him, but what a saintly man he is . . ." I left. Half an hour later, the priest came out pale and discombobulated, wiping the sweat

FRANCO ON SANTA'S LAP

from his forehead. "Good night, Father," I said. But he could hardly answer me. I entered the room, and Franco had a seraphic smile on his face, a renewed peace, satisfied with his last act.

As if this were not enough, he managed to give me one last "rigor mortis" of embarrassment after his death. It happened when I realized I no longer knew where his ashes were. He's not at the Pincetto. He left so many instructions about what to do with him that I think we lost him. That might seem horrible to you, but I've concluded that this is the kind of burial that suits Franco best—embarrassing us from wherever he is, and forever.

"Stop, Isabella, that's enough!" I can hear *i miei morti* in a chorus of protest. "Stop talking about

Franco, his ashes, his soul, and what he did. You're ready to de-fame and slander any family member for your pleasure of exag-geration." Okay, I'll say no more . . . I don't know that I'm exaggerating. . . . But, yes, there's always the possibility that I made it all up. Maybe I should admit to lying about losing Franco and save my family from public disgrace.

ZIA MARCELLA AND THE BEYOND

When my Aunt Marcella was old, I made her promise that when she died—and now she has—she would give me a sign if there was any kind of afterlife: a dream, a metaphysical sign, any-thing. I would be on the alert. I feel now that something is sit-ting in my brain. I don't know how it got there, but I know it has something to do with Zia Marcella keeping her promise to me. The translation of this sensation into a conversation goes:

ZIA MARCELLA: YOU THINK WE WERE AND ARE NO MORE, AND THIS SAD-DENS YOU. YOU SENSE THE PAST, THE PRESENT, THE FUTURE—IT'S THE LIM-ITATION OF YOUR HUMAN PERCEPTION. THERE IS NO SUCH TIME. YOU CANNOT REALLY SAY WE WERE AND ARE NO MORE.

ISABELLA: ARE YOU NOW?

ZIA MARCELLA: AREN'T WE WITH YOU ALWAYS?

ISABELLA: ONLY THROUGH MY IMAGINARY CONVERSATIONS WITH ALL OF YOU DEAD ONES. IS THE PROOF OF THE BEYOND, THE AFTERLIFE, AS SILLY AND SIMPLE AS THIS?

ZIA MARCELLA: WHY NOT? BIG QUESTIONS MAY HAVE SIMPLE ANSWERS.

ISABELLA: YOU ARE NO MORE. I INVENT CONVERSATIONS WITH YOU TO ALLE-VIATE MY LOSS.

ZIA MARCELLA: I WOULDN'T DISMISS WHAT YOU DO SO EASILY. DON'T BE-

LITTLE YOUR HUMANITY, AND DON'T BE FOOLED BY IT, EITHER. YOU SAY THE
PAST IS NO MORE BECAUSE IT NO LONGER EXISTS.

ISABELLA: CORRECT.

ZIA MARCELLA: BUT THE SAME CAN BE SAID FOR THE FUTURE. THE FU-
TURE, BEING NOT YET, DOESN'T EXIST.

ISABELLA: RIGHT.

ZIA MARCELLA: CAN YOU FEEL THE PRESENT?

ISABELLA: YES, I CAN.

ZIA MARCELLA: HOW CAN YOU FEEL ANYTHING EXISTING BETWEEN TWO
THINGS THAT DON'T EXIST?

Luciano, my philosopher friend, always intervenes in my
imagination during conversations of this type. These are the
kinds of ideas he routinely occupies himself with.

LUCIANO: YOUR AUNT IS RIGHT. EINSTEIN TELLS US ABOUT THE PARADOX OF
THE TWINS. ONCE UPON A TIME THERE WERE TWIN BROTHERS WHO FOR
TWENTY YEARS SPENT ALL THEIR TIME TOGETHER—SCHOOL, HOLIDAYS,
PARTIES, THEY WERE INSEPARABLE. THEN ONE DAY ONE GETS A JOB AS A
CLERK IN A BANK. THE OTHER BOARDS A SPACESHIP AND FLIES AMONG THE
STARS. TWENTY YEARS LATER, FEELING NOSTALGIC FOR HIS BROTHER, HE
COMES HOME TO EARTH. HE FINDS HIS BROTHER, AT FORTY YEARS OLD, TO
HAVE BEEN PROMOTED TO DIRECTOR OF THE BANK. BUT HE, THE ASTRO-
NAUT TWIN, IS ONLY TWENTY-ONE YEARS OF AGE. WHY? ACCORDING TO
EINSTEIN, IF YOU MOVE AT A HIGH ENOUGH SPEED, TIME SLOWS DOWN
UNTIL IT STOPS.

ISABELLA: I DON'T THINK EINSTEIN SAID SUCH THINGS. I DON'T KNOW WHAT
HE SAID, BUT IT MUST HAVE BEEN SOMETHING BETTER THAN THAT. IF YOU
WANT TO KEEP CALLING YOURSELF A PHILOSOPHER, YOU SHOULD STOP MAK-
ING SUCH IDIOTIC STATEMENTS.

LUCIANO: BUT HE DID SAY IT. IT'S YOU WHO ARE IGNORANT.

ISABELLA: YOU MEAN IF I START RUNNING AS FAST AS I CAN, I'LL STOP GROW-
ING OLD?

LUCIANO: YES. VERY FAST. YOU HAVE TO REACH AT LEAST THE SPEED OF LIGHT—186,000 MILES PER SECOND.

ISABELLA: HALLELUJAH! LANCÔME, STOP LAB RESEARCH ON ANTIWRINKLE CREAM AND JUST FIND A WAY TO MAKE US LADIES RUN FAST!

LUCIANO: THE CLOSEST STAR TO OUR EARTH IS ALPHA CENTAURI. IT'S FOUR LIGHT-YEARS AWAY FROM US. EVEN IF WE COULD FIND A WAY TO GO AS FAST AS LIGHT, A PHONE CONVERSATION TO ALPHA CENTAURI WOULD GO: "HELLO." FOUR YEARS TO GET THERE. FOUR YEARS FOR THE ANSWER TO COME BACK: "WHO IS IT?" "LUCIANO." FOUR YEARS TO GO. "HOW ARE YOU?" FOUR YEARS TO COME BACK. JUST THAT SHORT CONVERSATION WOULD TAKE SIXTEEN YEARS OF OUR TIME.

GRANDMOTHER ELETTRA, WITH MY FATHER, MY UNCLE, AND ZIA MARCELLA

ZIA MARCELLA: LUCIANO, PLEASE, HELP ME MAKE ISABELLA UNDERSTAND THAT. ETERNITY IS NOT THE ENDLESS SUCCESSION OF CENTURIES AS SHE THINKS, BUT TIME THAT DOESN'T MOVE.

ISABELLA: WHAT'S THIS NOW?

LUCIANO: ISABELLA, YOU WON'T UNDERSTAND IT, NOR WILL YOU HAVE THE PATIENCE TO LEARN MORE. WE ALL HAVE TO LIVE TO DIFFERENT DEGREES WITH THE UNANSWERABLE QUESTIONS. THE MORE YOU QUESTION, THE MORE QUESTIONS YOU HAVE.

And here Luciano starts to torment me with one of his philosophical litanies.

LUCIANO (CONTINUED): FOR ME, THE QUESTION MARK IS THE SYMBOL OF ALL THAT IS GOOD. THE EXCLAMATION POINT, ON THE OTHER HAND, IS THE SYMBOL OF BAD. THE QUESTION MARK IS KIND, OPEN TO DISCUSSION, READY FOR CHANGE, MOSTLY DEMOCRATIC. THE EXCLAMATION POINT IS DANGEROUS, RIGID, INTRANSIGENT, THE BASIS OF A LOT OF CLASHES, WARS, AND CONFLICT. YOU ARE A CREATURE OF ORDER, AND FOR THAT REASON

YOU WILL ALWAYS HAVE CONFLICT. . . . LOOK AT THE MEN YOU FALL IN LOVE WITH.

ISABELLA: WHAT ABOUT THEM?

LUCIANO: MONSTERS.

ISABELLA: ELETTRA'S DAD IS MORE THAN HANDSOME.

LUCIANO: I'M NOT TALKING ABOUT THEIR PHYSICAL ASPECTS, BUT FROM A HUMAN POINT OF VIEW. WASN'T GARY ALWAYS PLAYING ALL SORTS OF VILLAINS, FROM DRACULA TO THE TROUBLED SID VICIOUS, FROM LEE HARVEY OSWALD TO—

ISABELLA: THAT HAS NOTHING TO DO WITH GARY AS A MAN. AN ACTOR CAN BE A SAINT IN ONE FILM AND A MURDERER IN THE NEXT. IT DOESN'T MEAN HE HAS TO BE A SAINT OR AN ASSASSIN IN LIFE. BESIDES, HE'S ALSO BEEN BEETHOVEN.

LUCIANO: BUT IF HE WAS CHOSEN TO PORTRAY TYPES LIKE DRACULA, THERE MUST BE A VERY GOOD REASON. YOU SEE, BETWEEN ORDER AND DISORDER THERE HAS ALWAYS BEEN A GREAT ATTRACTION. YOU OBVIOUSLY BELONG TO THE WORLD OF ORDER, PROBABLY THANKS TO YOUR MOTHER, WHO, BEING SWEDISH, MUST HAVE BEEN INCREDIBLY ORDERLY. I'VE OBSERVED YOU FOR MANY YEARS. AT WORK YOU'RE ALWAYS VERY PREPARED, PUNCTUAL—"VERY PROFESSIONAL," AS THESE QUALITIES ARE GENERALLY REFERRED TO. SOMETIMES YOU LOOKED TO ME A LITTLE APPREHENSIVE—*TOO* ATTENTIVE, *TOO* EAGER, AS IF YOU WERE AFRAID SOMEONE WAS GOING TO SCOLD YOU.

ISABELLA: I DON'T LIKE BEING SCOLDED. I'LL DO ANYTHING TO PREVENT ANY KIND OF SCOLDING.

LUCIANO: YOU ARE A "CREATURE OF ORDER," AND YOUR DESTINY WILL ALWAYS BE TO FALL IN LOVE WITH MEN OF DISORDER.

ISABELLA: I DON'T KNOW WHAT YOU'RE TALKING ABOUT. I JUST LIKE UNPREDICTABLE, ORIGINAL PEOPLE.

LUCIANO: C'MON, ISABELLA, YOU KNOW WHAT I MEAN. I'D SAY YOU LIKE MORE THAN "ORIGINAL"—I'D CALL THEM FAR-OUT ECCENTRICS, AND IT'S NOT THEIR KINDNESS AND HUMANITY YOU RESPOND TO. I'D BE AFRAID TO

INTRODUCE YOU TO JACK THE RIPPER—YOU'D DRAG HIM INTO YOUR BED INSTANTLY. NOW LISTEN TO ME—THERE'S A REASON FOR THIS BEHAVIOR OF YOURS. IF I PUT A LITTLE BIT OF MILK INTO A CUP WITH A LITTLE BIT OF COFFEE, WHAT DO I GET?

ISABELLA: CAFÉ AU LAIT.

LUCIANO: RIGHT. AND WHY IS THAT SO?

ISABELLA: THAT'S HOW YOU MAKE CAFÉ AU LAIT.

LUCIANO: IT'S BECAUSE NATURE WILL ALWAYS TEND TOWARD AMALGAMA-TION. SO THAT THE MOLECULES OF COFFEE AND MILK ENTERING THE CUP DON'T STAY FACING EACH OTHER LIKE SOLDIERS OF OPPOSING ARMIES, BUT MIX. AND ONCE THEY MIX, THEY WILL NEVER GO BACK TO WHAT THEY WERE. A CAPPUCCINO CONTRIBUTES TO THE RATE OF DISORDER, AND IT'S IRRE-VERSIBLE. THAT'S THE TENDENCY OF THE UNIVERSE.

ISABELLA: I FALL IN LOVE WITH THESE TYPES OF GUYS BECAUSE THE UNI-VERSE TENDS INEVITABLY TO MIX, AND FROM ORDER I CREATE DISORDER?

LUCIANO: THE UNIVERSE ONE DAY WILL BECOME LIKE AN ENORMOUS CAP-PUCCINO. SOONER OR LATER, MATTER WILL DISAPPEAR. EVERYTHING WILL BE A UNIQUE MESS—EVEN PROTONS WON'T SUCCEED IN MAINTAINING THEIR INTEGRITY. . . . THERE WILL BE NO DIFFERENCES IN TEMPERATURE, ELECTROMAGNETIC OR GRAVITATIONAL FORCES. . . . THERE WILL BE NO REASON FOR MATTER . . .

. . . and on he goes. Do not believe that Luciano is only in-dulging himself in pure philosophical thoughts. Apart from all our ethereal exchanges, we had an affair, a physical event. I was in my early twenties, he in his early fifties. I said, "Luciano, you're the oldest lover I've ever had." He answered, "You, too," so you know that in spite of being up there in the higher sphere of philosophy, he is very much trapped in being a man. If you were to ask him now, "Do you find Isabella an appealing, beau-tiful woman?" he'd answer, "Is she a woman?" Our relationship has become, as Luciano puts it, "man to man." When we had our affair—man to woman—his editor used to beg me, "Make him suffer. The lobster effect works with him." According to the lobster effect, the meat is tastier with suffering. The animal has to be put into the boiling water alive. When Luciano suffers, he becomes a better philosopher. To evade the painful reality, he indulges in the big questions. Being young and cruel, I contribute to his escape to higher spheres. "Why do we exist?" "What is the universe?" "What is eternity?" "Does God exist?" But Luciano generally finds no answers.

LUCIANO: SO WHAT? I BELIEVE IN THE SCHOOL OF THOSE WHO SEARCH BUT FIND NOTHING.

ISABELLA: YOU JOINED A SAD CLUB.

LUCIANO: NOT AT ALL. THE JOY IS NOT AT THE SUMMIT, BUT IN THE CLIMB— OTHERWISE, ANY ALPINIST WOULD JUST ASK TO BE DROPPED ON THE TOP OF THE MOUNTAIN BY HELICOPTER.

ISABELLA: DON'T YOU THINK IT'S FAITH THAT ALLOWS MEN TO GO FORWARD? THE CONVICTION OF OUR BELIEFS?

LUCIANO: NOT FAITH, DOUBT—THE BASIS OF CURIOSITY, WHICH IS THE DRIVING POWER. THAT'S WHY I WORSHIP THE QUESTION MARK.

ISABELLA: IS MY IMAGINATION UNREAL, OR IS IT THE HIGHER TRUTH? DO YOU THINK THERE'S AN AFTERLIFE? OR NOTHINGNESS?

LUCIANO: THIS IS THE QUESTION THAT DRIVES ME THE LEAST TO FIND AN ANSWER. ALL I HAVE TO DO IS RELAX AND WAIT AND IN A FEW YEARS I'LL KNOW THE TRUTH. IF GOD EXISTS . . . DOES IT FOR YOU?

ISABELLA: MAYBE.

LUCIANO: THEN WHAT WAS HE DOING BEFORE HE CREATED THE UNIVERSE?

ISABELLA: ???

ZIA MARCELLA: A CHINESE PROVERB SAYS THE SKY IS TINTED BLUE BY ALL THE SIGHS WE EMANATE WITH THESE UNANSWERABLE QUESTIONS OF OURS.

ISABELLA: ZIA, PLEASE HELP ME, I HAVE A QUESTION. HOW DO I END THIS BOOK? I THOUGHT I COULD WRITE—

ZIA MARCELLA: It's a waste of time to find an "end," because there are no such things as "ends." You realize that consequently there are no beginnings either. You've already written a useless beginning.

ISABELLA: So what do I do? Do I finish and start the book in the middle of a sentence?

ZIA MARCELLA: That seems more appropriate to me.

I tell you, these *monstres sacrés* as they are called in French—these bigger-than-life creatures that make up my family—are "monsters" in other ways than "sacred." For one thing, their yakking in my head can be exhausting, and they interfere with everything. I have to deal with eternity, our earthly eternity. Not my aunt's eternity, the one that lets her toy with and scramble my brain, but the real one, the one that confronted me when my parents died. My sisters, brothers, and I had to deal with something unusual: history, and what to do with it.

OUR EARTHLY ETERNITY

Is being remembered a kind of antidote to death? Is fame a sort of eternity? A remedy to the sadness of the end? Does having a famous mother, who is still seen every day on TV smiling, crying, walking, talking, make her death different, less definitive than other deaths? What about Father? Since he was a director, we don't see him or hear him, but his films are shown. His beliefs, thoughts, mind are displayed on TV and in retrospectives of his work. Is his presence more alive than that of other dead mortals? I do my imaginary conversations more often with my father

My cousin Geppy's
sculpture of
my father

and mother than with my other dead ones, but is that so only because they are my parents, or has their fame created a live presence for me?

Watching my dad's films has a healing power for me. At first, just after his death, I couldn't see them because it hurt too much. Then I started to watch them with my brother Renzo during the anguished months and sleepless nights when we were waiting for Lisa to come out of her coma.

Lisa was one of my best friends whom my eldest brother, Renzo, married. They were together in a car that was bumped and pushed off the road by another car speeding on the freeway. Both were severely injured, my brother with broken ribs, femur, and vertebrae, and punctured lungs and heart. Lisa, who looked untouched, was in fact the more gravely wounded, with a deep brain injury, her body slowly curling and locking into the fetal position that was the sign of the gravity of her state. We feared she would remain a vegetable, but a more dramatic fate was reserved for her. Coming out of her coma, she was diagnosed as having a "locked-in" syndrome. This is when a conscious mind can receive all inputs from the outside world but can't respond to any of them. The mind is like a two-way street—one lane for input, the other lane for output. In Lisa, the output lane was severed; she had no voluntary functions. She couldn't talk, walk, smile, move. Only her reflexes were left intact, allowing her to stay alive. A function such as swallowing worked as a reflex, preventing her from choking on her own saliva, but not if she had to swallow food and drink because that requires a voluntary movement. She could blink only one eye. Eye movements are not funneled through the same "two-way street" part of the brain through which all other commands have to pass. Lisa could answer our questions by blinking her right eye; the left eye had been blinded in the car accident. She would blink once for "Yes" and twice for "No." That eye expressed all the alertness and intelligence of a conscious mind as well as all her desperation. The power of her feelings was concentrated in that eye, which became incredibly telling—a true window to her soul. It was as though that soul were trapped inside her body, unable to fly away and follow whatever destiny is reserved for us when we die. She lived in this dramatic state for five months, until death was granted to her.

It was during these months that Renzo and I started to watch our dad's films. It was the only activity besides being at Lisa's bedside that could engage us. It was a little like being with him, feeling his paternal warmth, his joy in life, his hope. Dad had approached the drama of war with such compassion, tenderness, and affection, it seemed to us an indication of how we might survive our own tragedies. Through his films he was still able to exert his paternal guidance.

Dad's essence could be found in his work; I have not found mother's essence in hers. I can catch only glimpses of her true self in her movies. Maybe this is so because a film is more the creation of a director than of an actor, or simply because my mom's job was, after all, to pretend being someone else. She succeeded at it, as we know, brilliantly.

I cannot watch my mother's later work. It's the way I remember her, and her image—too vivid on screen—hurts. I can watch the earlier work done in Sweden or Hollywood because I never knew my mother so young. I was born after those glorious years of her career. The easiest film to watch is *Casablanca*, which has become such an icon that it has acquired a distance for me; by sheer overexposure it has lost the power to aim a dart at my heart. I even drink my morning cappuccino in a *Casablanca* cup.

MY DAUGHTER'S SCULPTURE OF MY MOTHER

It feels like affectionately teasing my mother about this other expression of the immortal memory she left of herself: T-shirts, postcards, dishware with her image on them. I find this private joke between me and her spirit a good way of starting my day.

To this day it is the voice that has the most power to move me. A familiar intonation can go through me and bring me to tears. One day, watching a documentary on Anna Magnani's life, I came upon an unexpected interview with Father taken from some archive. Seeing him shocked me, but hearing his voice made my head spin; I felt I was going to faint. It took a long time to come out of a kind of daze—the same daze I feel when I visit my mother's archive.

My sisters and brothers and I decided to assemble all the material we could find about our parents. Since Mother was organized and orderly and Father disorganized and disorderly, there is much more of her than of him at the Jeanine Basinger Cinema Archive at Wesleyan University in Connecticut. We donated letters, scripts, photos, newspaper articles, diaries, costumes. At the start of this big project, I would call Jeanine and ask, "I found a pad with my mother's list of groceries to buy. Is this history, or shall I throw it away?" She'd say, "We don't know yet. Our duty is to keep things long enough to allow history to make that decision. A grocery list a millennium old could be quite interesting."

The conservation and restoration of my parents' films is a much bigger project. My family and I do as much as we can, but financially, legally, and practically it's a major undertaking. Films can be preserved only through the intervention of the big Hollywood studios and government institutions.

In 1979, while I was married to Martin Scorsese, he realized that films were literally fading away. Martin is a big film scholar and spends most of his day either making films or watching them. Watching old films, he realized that prints that were only ten years old had faded, turning into one color: magenta. Investigating film archives, he was among the first to realize that different film stocks had different survival rates, and all of them were deteriorating fast. Color film stock from the fifties and sixties, which cost less so that films no longer had to be made in black and white, was found to be the most volatile. Fifty percent of the color films made in those years are estimated to be lost already. And nitrate prints of the oldest films, from the beginning of this art form through the forties, are highly inflammable, and nowhere near all of them have as yet been transferred to safer stock. The independently produced films seem to be the most vulnerable. These are often the most artistic, most avant-garde work, but having no financial backing in the way of a structured film studio, they're often not even collected on the shelves of neglectful vaults and laboratories. The companies that produce these films often have a short existence, leaving either no trace or a confused record of legal rights and the whereabouts of the negatives.

Martin started a big campaign, with a strength and determination that matches that of the Christian crusaders of the twelfth and thirteenth centuries, to raise awareness that this art form, which has so influenced our century, will leave no trace of itself in the next centuries if something isn't done.

I remember my mother late one night standing alone on the stage of the Haymarket Theatre in London. It was the last evening she had performed in *Waters of the Moon* by N. C. Hunter. She melancholically said to me, "All this talent—the set, the costumes, the lighting, and us, the actors—all gone. Not to be seen by anyone ever again. It's so sad. Thank God for films—at least that expression of talent can be enjoyed by people in many countries for many years to come." I know now that she was wrong.

I once saw two Tibetan monks in the window of the IBM Building on Madison Avenue in New York. Working day after day, they created a sand sculpture of intricate spiritual drawings and different colors and shapes, a mandala. It was an anachronistic setup, and it fascinated me. The day the last touch completed their work, they destroyed it with one gesture and walked away. It was a reminder that everything is impermanent. That gesture of destruction was meant to symbolize the eventual destruction of everything in the universe.

At the premiere of *Little Buddha* at the Berlin Film Festival, I was sitting next to Bernardo Bertolucci, the film's director. At the end of the film, Bernardo leaned over to me and said, "That's why I have doubts about film restoration. Isn't everything destined to end anyway? Aren't we wiser just to resign ourselves to it and learn from Buddhism that everything is impermanent?"

"Why did you save all these letters, photos, and diaries?" I asked my mother as I watched her busying herself in the small storage room of her London apartment, organizing the bulk of what became, after her death, the Ingrid Bergman Archive. My mother was dying, and she knew it. Her reaction to this, as it had been to everything else in life, was to clean everything and leave things orderly. "I always knew I was going to be famous" was her answer. I was shocked by it. It seemed such an arrogant answer, and I did not want my mommy to be arrogant, so I asked no more. I never told this story to anyone. I didn't want anybody to think my mother could be arrogant. Then, with the years and the process of beatification that all dead people go through, becoming better in our memories than they were in life, I began to question myself. I must have misunderstood what Mother said, I told myself. I know she wasn't arrogant, I should have just asked her to repeat herself. Stupid me. Why didn't I? I'd known she wasn't going to live long. I knew I wouldn't have another opportunity.

I confided my regrets to Jeanine Basinger, the curator of Mother's archive. "You didn't misunderstand her," said Jeanine. "She knew she was going to be famous. She wrote it in her diary when she was fourteen years old."

Shocked even more deeply, I called my friend Yasmine Ergas. She is "my most intelligent friend"—this is how I always introduce her, for her indisputable brilliance. "Isn't it phenomenal that my mother always knew she was going to be famous?" "Lots of people believe that about themselves and keep detailed records of their lives, only most of them don't become famous" was Yasmine's matter-of-fact answer, demolishing my astonishment that was already leading me to uncover yet another supernatural phenomenon in my family.

I know that most filmmakers, not only my mother, believe their work is here to stay. For how long? Forever? Or for "some time" after their deaths? And this "some time"—how long is it? A few generations?

If Hollywood were not in California but in Tibet, the fading of films might have been celebrated as a spiritual teaching. I come from Rome, the "Eternal City," which is full of art made not of sand but of marble, intended to challenge time and last forever. I gave way to my culture and collected and conserved my parents' work. Martin's imaginary voice supports this choice of mine.

MARTIN: EVERYTHING HAS TO GO, OKAY. BUT WHY NOW? I LOVE TO SEE THE COLOSSEUM, VERSAILLES, THE PYRAMIDS—CAN WE MAKE FILMS LAST A LITTLE LONGER FOR OTHER GENERATIONS TO SEE THEM? I LEARNED FILM-MAKING BY WATCHING THE OLD MASTERS. YOUNG DIRECTORS WILL WANT TO DO THE SAME. WE HAVE TO PRESERVE FILMS FOR THEM, AND IN THE BEST CONDITION.

HOW CAN YOU STUDY FILMS BY WATCHING VIDEOS ON A SMALL TV SCREEN OR HORRIBLE BEATEN-UP PRINTS LIKE THE ONES THAT CIRCULATE ON COLLEGE CAMPUSES? MEDICAL STUDENTS DON'T STUDY MEDICINE ON DECAYING, ROTTING CORPSES OR ON PIGS' AND DOGS' BODIES BECAUSE THEY APPROXIMATE HUMAN BODIES. WE HAVE TO PRESERVE FILMS WELL—WHICH FILMS I DON'T KNOW. ALL OF THEM. REMEMBER, A SUCCESSFUL FILM OF TODAY MAY NOT BE THE ONE SELECTED BY HISTORY. THINK OF VAN GOGH.

My dad's films were not successful commercially when they came out and acquired a unique historical meaning only with time. *Open City* and *Paisan* are not only artistic statements but also powerful documents of World War II. My father would have enjoyed the justice time has rendered him.

MARTIN (CONTINUED): EVERYTHING HAS TO BE SAVED . . . INTENTIONALLY OR UNINTENTIONALLY, BY FIRES, FLOODS, WARS, ANGER, MERE SPITE, AN IR-RATIONAL GESTURE OF DISCOURAGEMENT . . . WHO KNOWS WHAT CAN HAP-PEN. MORE IS LOST THAN IS KEPT. SAVE EVERYTHING, SO THAT A LITTLE WILL REMAIN.

November 1, 1996: Tatto, the new kitten I got at the ASPCA, shat on my *Blue Velvet* wig. For ten years I kept that wig as a personal memory of the film and for posterity, if it was interested. Today I had to throw the wig away. I am pissed off. As usual, Martin is right.